KING PENGUIN

TOM AND VI...

Michael Hastings was born in 1938, and brought up in Brixton where he still lives. At fifteen he commenced a three-year apprenticeship in bespoke tailoring. And in 1956, George Devine invited Hastings to join the Royal Court Theatre as an actor/writer. He has also written five novels – *The Game* (1957), *The Frauds* (1959), *Tussy is Me* (1968), *The Nightcomers* (1971) and *And in the Forest the Indians* (1975); a collection of short stories, *Bart's Mornings and Other Tales of Modern Brazil* (1975); and two biographies, *Rupert Brooke: The Handsomest Young Man in England* (1969) and *Sir Richard Burton* (1978).

His plays are: *Don't Destroy Me*, directed by Robert Peake, 1956; *Yes and After*, directed by John Dexter, 1957; *The World's Baby*, directed by Patrick Dromgoole, 1964; *For the West (Congo)*, directed by Toby Robertson, 1965; *Blue as His Eyes the Tin Helmet He Wore*, directed by David Cunliffe, 1966; *Lee Harvey Oswald: 'a far mean streak of indepence brought on by negleck'*, directed by Peter Coe, 1967; *The Silence of Saint-Just*, directed by Walter Eyselink, 1972; *The Cutting of the Cloth*, unperformed autobiographic play, 1973; *For the West (Uganda)*, directed by Nicholas Wright, 1977; *Gloo Joo*, directed by Michael Rudman, 1978; *Full Frontal*, directed by Rufus Collins, 1979; *Carnival War*, directed by Antonia Bird, 1979; *Gloo Joo*, TV, directed by John Kaye Cooper, 1979; *Murder Rap*, TV, directed by Peter Duffell, 1980; *Midnight at the Starlight*, directed for .... 1980; *Midnite at the Starlite*, d............... gham Studio Theatre; *Tom a*............... 1984; and *Stars of the Roller S*............... BBC, 1984, and for the Brixt...

Michael Hastings ha............... demy of Arts and Sciences 'Emmy', the Somerset Maugham Award, the *Evening Standard* Comedy of the Year, BAFTA and Writers' Guild awards. He was the subject of a programme in the BBC's Writers and Places series, entitled *Michael Hastings in Brixton*, directed by Sandra Gregory, 1980.

TOM AND VIV

Michael Hastings

A KING PENGUIN PUBLISHED BY
PENGUIN BOOKS

Penguin Books Ltd, Harmondsworth, Middlesex, England
Viking Penguin Inc., 40 West 23rd Street, New York, New York 10010, U.S.A.
Penguin Books Australia Ltd, Ringwood, Victoria, Australia
Penguin Books Canada Ltd, 2801 John Street, Markham, Ontario, Canada L3R 1B4
Penguin Books (N.Z.) Ltd, 182–190 Wairau Road, Auckland 10, New Zealand

First published by The Royal Court Theatre 1984
Published with an Introduction in Penguin Books 1985

The performing rights of this play
are fully protected, and permission
to perform must be obtained in
advance from Jonathan Clowes Ltd,
19 Jeffrey's Place, London NW1 9PP

Made and printed in Great Britain by
Richard Clay (The Chaucer Press) Ltd,
Bungay, Suffolk
Filmset in Monophoto Palatino by
Northumberland Press Ltd, Gateshead,
Tyne and Wear

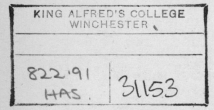

'Vivie drew this punt at Oxford shortly before they wed. Tom's Bloomsbury bunch called her "the river girl". They were afraid of her; they
destroyed her.' – Maurice Haigh-Wood

CONTENTS

ACKNOWLEDGEMENTS

Acknowledgements to the Texas University Library, Austin; McMaster University Library, Hamilton, Ontario; Berg Collections, New York Public Library; Bodleian Library, Oxford.

And to: friends and relatives of Louise Purdon; the matron of Northumberland House (1945–65), who wishes to remain anonymous; Mrs Isabelle Lockyer for a detailed interview; relatives of Dr Reginald Miller; the surviving members of the Schiff family; Sir Sacheverel Sitwell; Dora Russell, and Shirlene Todd Backus, of Turdus Gorge, Wyoming; and the kind and detailed medical summaries and advice from Professor Derek Russell Davis. And further medical commentary from Dr Alexander Walk, Dr Eliot Slater, Dr Rudolph Freudenberg and Dr David Clark. A word of thanks to Edith Morgan, Mary Appleby, Annie Gatti for her indefatigible research, and Allen & Hanbury's archives.

I am further indebted to Herbert Howarth (*Notes on Some Figures behind T. S. Eliot*), Lyndall Gordon (*Eliot's Early Years*) and Yale University library.

Throughout the rehearsal work process, the Royal Court Company's own contribution included certain ruthless razor-sharp editing by Tom Wilkinson and Julie Covington; a restructuring of Louise Purdon's character, after further checks with Allen & Hanbury, and the details of Louise's commitment to the National Society for Lunacy Law Reform by Deborah Findlay; and Nicholas Selby's illuminating work on Rose Haigh-Wood's fascination with Japanese wallpaper, and Margaret Tyzack's clever reworking of original Rose Haigh-Wood correspondence into her speeches.

Victoria Hardie made substantial contributions to Parts One, Three and Five, when, in particular, I was quite unable to make accurate devolution of a scene from a female character's point of view.

NOTE

I interviewed Colonel Maurice Haigh-Wood over five months in 1980, the year he died. I am also indebted to the remaining members of his family, Mildred Haigh-Wood, and the Colonel's grandchildren Jane and Ann. A member of the Hoagland family, Judge White, provided some kind guidance. Most studies in Eliot have encountered degrees of animosity and obstructiveness from Faber & Faber and the Eliot estate, and I certainly am not alone in this matter; nevertheless, given time and patience and understanding and belief in the greater good via sharing information, these unusual situations will not prevail. Meanwhile, a thousand or so letters in the Emily Hale file at Princeton are under embargo until 2020. The Mary Trevelyan diaries which refer to the 1940s are at present withheld. And the John Hayward papers at Cambridge are only available to a select few. The Hope Mirrlees documents, which were sold off at various times, are scattered in a number of American universities, and proper collation has not been attempted. The same applies to the Lucy Thayer/Scofield Thayer material (1908–22), some of which remains in the possession of two families.

A significant problem attaches itself to the papers of Vivienne Haigh-Wood. At the time of her internment all rights of identity, passport, bank accounts, insurance contributions, possessions and even clothing were stripped from her. She had no means of redress, and such items as family pictures, personal keepsake trivia, photographs and incidental family silver, and carpets and books were promptly placed out of her legal reach. Her income from the Haigh-Wood estate was handed on to the authority of the official family trustees. The thorniest problem remains the right of attachment on her papers and documents; according to her own notes there are at least ten short stories, a number of poems, a number of review pieces and some further sketches.

According to her brother, Maurice, there are many more diaries which she kept up, and a number of letters she wrote to Eliot from the asylum over a period of ten years. There is, in addition, a small library of books which Tom and Viv gathered out of their own shared interests. From Vivienne's final will − bearing in mind the more recent rulings on copyright in unpublished material − the indications are that all her papers remain the property of the Bodleian Library. The Bodleian has not exercised this right, although it has insisted nothing from the five diaries in its possession may be used for any form of fiction. The Bodleian, it is hoped, will one day implement this apparent right and seek access and attachment to these papers wherever they may be found.

'At some point in their marriage Tom went mad, and promptly certified his wife.'

Edith Sitwell

'He never stopped writing about Vivienne until *The Confidential Clerk*, and that was 1953.'

'He had this deep nostalgia for a closed hierarchic society ... this Edwardian upper-middle-class family ... really! ...'

Rebecca West

'I think he bit off more than he could chew. He didn't understand the rules, actually. You see – you have to be kind to Vivie.'

Maurice Haigh-Wood

'She is dead but sings anyway.' (Stage notes for *The Sad Lament of Pecos Bill on the Eve of Killing his Wife*.)

Sam Shepard

INTRODUCTION

In the theatre all biography is fiction, and some fiction is autobiography. The idea of omniscient narrative in straightforward
biography doesn't apply to the stage. No play can delineate
factual substance of the years, or spell out circumstance, all this
belongs to the book. What a play can achieve is to take time past
and time present and thread it through the needle of the years
and provide the audience with a pictorial statement. For
example, there is a scene in my play *Tom and Viv* where the
mother, the brother and the husband attend a Magistrate's Court
during an application for Viv's internment to an asylum. In
reality these three did not of course meet in the Court; in
essential truth no three people were more responsible for this
application for an internment. So one can see at a glance this is
not traditional biography, but what is it?

I asked a radical feminist what she would do with the material
for the play *Tom and Viv*. She had no hesitation: 'If I'd written
that play, Tom would have gone to jail for life for his male
characteristics. Viv would have written *The Waste Land* and
become the most famous poet of the century. She later married
Oswald Mosley and turned the offices of Faber & Faber into a
printshop for the British Union of Fascists. And she and Mosley
had four daughters – Marghanita Laski, Myra Hindley, Ruth Ellis
and Margaret Thatcher. Then, around 1960 Viv won the Nobel
Peace Prize. Her kids quarantined the adult male population
following compulsory sterilization. All other males under age
were subject to curfew laws. Shortly after her death at a great
age, a female Pope would promptly canonize Viv.' I don't want
to dwell on this gay fanfaronade; the point she makes is that at
times to reclaim the past a different view is required.

Eliot's own view of biography was acute: 'We may also search
and snatch eagerly at any anecdote of private life which may

give us the feeling for a moment of seeing him as his contemporaries saw him. We may try to put the two together, peering through the obscurity of time for the unity which was both the mind in the masterpiece and the man of daily business; but failing this, we often relapse into stressing the differences between the two pictures. No one can be understood; but between a great artist of the past and a contemporary whom one has known as a friend there is the difference between a mystery which baffles and a mystery which is accepted. We cannot explain, but we accept and in a way understand.'

In the last twenty years I have found my own work breaking up into twin sections. There are private plays entirely in the realm of fiction. And there are public plays from which, in order to explore issues, familiar people emerge – Idi Amin, Richard Burton, Saint-Just, Lee Harvey Oswald, Tom Eliot and, in fictional prose, Eleanor Marx. In one instance, I took the central characters from the Henry James novella and led them to the first page of *The Turn of the Screw* in a short novel, *The Nightcomers* (1971). If life spares there are other plays underway on Marcus Garvey and the heroic rise of the Universal Negro Improvement Association, on Abie Warburg and his internment at the Kreutzlingen Institute, on Alfred Watkins's vision from Bredwardine, and on David Bomberg's work for the early Zionists in Palestine and his theory of 'spirit in mass'. In addition there is the occasional foray in the direction of *Rupert Brooke: The Handsomest Young Man in England* (1969). But what exactly is all this work in aid of?

As it happened, I was merrily floating down a river in the south-western corner of Brazil, state of Campo Grande, not long ago, doing my utmost to appear useful. And I found an answer to this question. My companion – an Italian who'd settled with his wife, Alice, in the forest – took me to a riverhead. At a point which indeed looked impenetrable, he explained that this was where the legendary Colonel Fawcett and his nephew vanished sixty years ago. But, according to my companion, there was no mystery. The *indios* knew exactly what had happened. The preposterous Colonel led his team into the forest, doubled back over his path, and made sure no one would ever follow him in. And if he did discover his 'city of seven pillars' he had no intention whatsoever of sharing the gold booty with the rest of us. Fawcett's life was incomplete without his mythical lost city in the trees. At home in my room I possibly recognized these same ghosts of mine, the Garveys and Watkinses and Oswalds and Eliots and Warburgs, as creatures of fragmentation; tense animals on a precipice clutching at icons, a wholeness of life observed but not found, as if we are, like them, flung into this century like gunshot particles, moving outwards at speed, this centre not holding, the wise declaring outrage, the stupid merely apathetic in Steiner's 'establishment of the mind'.

I've grown rather fond of Percy Harrison Fawcett. He made me tamp the lethargy. I've begun to ferret and stitch through my tiny world, shaking off outrage for the sake of it, or self-contempt in the name of inherited imperialisms; and discovered a sense of re-ordering these cultural ghosts. And by way of unexpectedly wild and dangerous alliances I had means of observing these ghosts as unfinished artifacts. Now I am drawn to them not in order to cut down, but to define the outermost edges of the minds, a distressed area, a frayed selvedge tether. An example of this more positive spirit is to be found in the story of Abie Warburg. He was confined to the asylum at Kreutzlingen in the early twenties. But Warburg was of the opinion he had regained his sanity. The doctors were not so convinced. For some months prior to internment, Warburg had been in Mexico. And at the asylum he made a fascinating bargain with the doctors. If he could deliver a lucid lecture on the ritual love dances of the Mexican rattlesnake to the doctors and inmates, they would release him. Warburg's gamble was to return from the broken mind, enlist the limitations and disciplines of his internment, and proceed to redefine the map of his potential. This great scholar wanted to return to the world, to his life of ideas, order of Mnemosyne and library of social memory. And far from subtracting his illness he was prepared to be judged by it. Far from concealing his fragmentation he decided to embrace it. And there are other alliances I believe I have found. How unusual to find

Trotsky describing Tolstoy as a kind of vessel filled with 'the anonymous massiveness of life and its sacred irresponsibility'. How ironic to discover that Gramsci, one who'd spent his adult years bearing intolerable pain, could call me to action with his phrase, adopted from Rolland, 'pessimism of the intellect, optimism of the will'. And I find I am now looking out for these ghosts, clamorous fingers on precipice ledges grasping at shards, and I start to feel like a man who's found a vase in fragments; and, for my sins, I have begun to put it back together. In Georg Lukács's words: 'Portray the age without giving way to despair.'

T. S. Eliot is undoubtedly one of the greatest poets of our century. A poet of such refined sensibilities, who freely ransacked cultural history to make the early poetry out of a form of collage. An acknowledged master magpie of modern letters. At the same time I noticed his characteristic of unhinging a part of himself, which was quite the opposite of Warburg, who was willing to embrace an entirety of self. But Eliot refined this in public. He found it necessary to detach his personality to surrender to writing. To achieve this characteristic of self-fragmenting meant burying sections of his pained and private life. Yet there were indications that this very same private life was the source of his finest work.

In 1979 I approached the Royal Court Theatre with the proposition that the distress Eliot experienced in his first marriage to Vivienne Haigh-Wood was a major influence on his poetry. The theatre kindly offered a commission with a view to perform the play for three weeks. And to provide some funds for a researcher. Four years later, and after a number of drafts of the play, it may be instructive to reflect a little on the reactions to the endeavour.

At the outset, Max Stafford-Clark, the Artistic Director of the theatre, wrote immediately to the Eliot estate. And was informed in a reply, dated February 1980, that we could have no access to material by or about Vivienne Haigh-Wood Eliot. This is not necessarily an unusual response to Eliot students. The bibliographer Donald Gallup was willing to collate all Vivienne's known writings: her stories published and unpublished, poems and review pieces from the *Criterion*, and related work she appeared to have contributed to the writing of *The Waste Land*. Gallup was not encouraged in this venture by the Eliot estate on the grounds that it would be difficult to separate and identify Tom or Viv's hand. The least this situation indicates is that the presence of Viv belongs in there, after all. The most one might find is that the two of them shared a life of some sort, no matter at what cost or pain, frequently shared the work process, and were partners to some degree. Eliot at one point during the making of *The Waste Land* was determined to wait upon Vivienne's judgement before he continued. It remains true that for certain Eliotians, only too eager to underscore his fear and hatred of the female body and its functions, and only too determined to apotheosize his later oath of chastity, this is something of an unpleasant paradox. Not only was he the poet who detached his personality in order to write, he was also the husband who announced: 'She has been ready to sacrifice everything for me. She has everything to give that I want, and she gives it. I owe her everything.'

Therefore, emboldened by the rebuff from the Eliot estate, I made approaches to Faber & Faber, in the person of Frank Morley, a director of the firm, and the figure most responsible for providing Eliot a shelter during the first agonized years of separation. After several attempts, I did achieve an exchange of sorts with a remarkably volatile figure. With care I explained the proposition of my play, but I detected an unusual tremor in his response:

'What a perfectly filthy idea!'

'I'm sorry?'

'What are you? A jerk, a twister, a scandalmaker?'

'No. I'm a playwright attached to the Royal Court Theatre, with which I've been associated for many years.'

'Are you out of your senses?'

'I hope not.'

'Has somebody put you up to this filth?'

'Filth?' I asked.

'Who is paying you?'

'I don't know if you'd call it actual payment. The commission at the Royal Court Theatre stands at £200 down, and a further £200 on delivery and acceptance of the play. Therefore I –'

'What academic qualifications have you?'

'None.'

'Where were you educated?'

'Here and there.'

'Are you in *Who's Who*?'

'I am in *Who's Who*, but I don't see what –'

'Since when!' Morley bellowed.

'I don't quite follow what that has to do with – well, for what it's worth, I've been in *Who's Who* since I was twenty-nine,' I replied.

Morley drew breath. Then he asked me in a conspiratorial tone: 'What do you know about 46 Broadhurst Gardens, the Hampstead episode? What do you know about 38 Burghley Mansions, and those goings on?'*

'Nothing whatsoever. Why, should I?'

I detected an element of relief. He demanded I put any questions I had in writing. Gave me his address to send to. I duly wrote off. But I never heard from him again. For a spell the theatre employed a respected researcher, Annie Gatti, to undertake initial work. I plodded off to the University of Texas, New York Public Library and a number of similar institutions in the States and in the U.K. In due course I wrote a letter to the scholar Dame Helen Gardner. She is a noted author of metaphysical dissertation who has over the past forty years written various studies of Eliot. Gardner replied, in a letter dated June 1981, that she didn't know anything about Vivienne Eliot, and if she did she wouldn't pass it on to me. Yours sincerely. Now this, from a scholar who'd already had privileged access to Eliot papers at the John Hayward Collection, Cambridge, which no other

---

* Viv's aunt Lillia lived at Broadhurst Gardens, directly behind the Haigh-Wood home. The house was a refuge for Viv during the breakdown of her first engagement. Unlike the rest of the family, Lillia Syme encouraged Tom and Viv to marry. Burghley Mansions, St Martin's Lane, was shared by C. H. B. Kitchin (1895–1967), Roger Senhouse (1900–1970) and Philip Ritchie (1899–1927).

person had been awarded, struck me as a little curt. There was emerging a uniformity in the animus, but I couldn't quite locate the origin of it.

There is a particularly intriguing diary of the late Mary Trevelyan, which gives a useful description of Eliot throughout the war years, this crucial time when Vivienne was placed in the asylum. This diary has not been published, and an author, Humphrey Carpenter, was fortunate enough to inherit this material. Over a period of two years, I made several applications to him for access to this diary, but was rejected each time. The last exchange I had with Carpenter ended abruptly. He said, 'This is an extremely sensitive area. Mrs Valerie Eliot will not stand for it. I have to abide by what she says.'

Among many other interviews, I had a talk with the writer Laurens van der Post. He was sympathetic to the proposition within the play, and genially added I should continue with the project no matter what. As for himself, he felt quite unable to talk about Tom and Viv: 'You see, I do not want in any way to jeopardize my relationship with the sole Eliot trustee, Valerie Eliot. Thank you, and goodbye.'

Suitably admonished, I trotted back to the amiable and patient Royal Court Theatre, and in my new role as a jeopard of modern letters I regaled Rob Ritchie, the literary manager, with prompt tidings of my forays, rueful and otherwise. But some good fortune was at hand. Our researcher, Annie Gatti, had found Viv's younger brother, Maurice Haigh-Wood. Colonel Haigh-Wood was near Bristol. He'd reluctantly ploughed through a book of mine, *Rupert Brooke: The Handsomest Young Man in England*, and informed us he'd be willing to meet the jeopard of Sloane Square.

Maurice, known as 'Haighie' to his old army friends, was in his eighty-fifth year, very attentive, rather curious, agreed to meet me every week or thereabouts on the cheerful understanding he didn't have to wade through any more of my books. He had less of an irascible nature, something more akin to a clipped good-humour: 'Reading books tremendous nuisance now. Anyway, want to die as soon as poss. And you will have to fetch

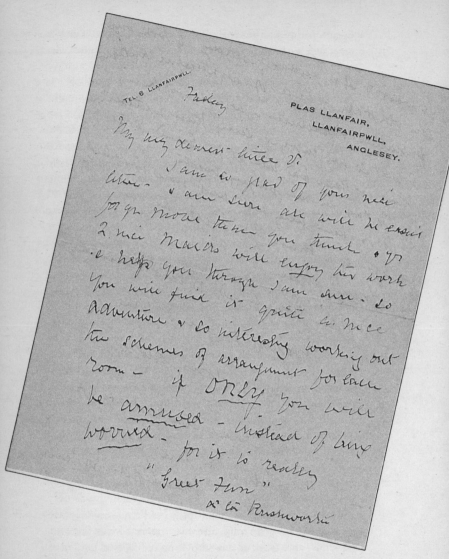

Letter from Rose Haigh-Wood to Vivienne, with reference to Tom and Viv's move to
Chester Terrace, 1928. 'My very dearest little V. I am so glad of your nice letter – & am
sure all will be easier for yr move than you think & yr 2 nice maids will *enjoy* their
work & help you through I am sure – so you will find it quite a nice adventure & so interesting
working out the schemes of arrangement for each room – if *only* you will be *amused* – instead
of being *worried* – for it is really "Great Fun" à la Rushworth ...'

and carry for me to the Onslow Court Hotel, London. I've got three trunks, a safe deposit, and half the family silver in the cellar downstairs. You can jolly well make yourself useful because I'll need some of the papers brought down.'

And so I visited the Colonel on a regular basis for five months – these proved to be the last five months of his life – and the old boy took to me with a mixture of weariness and calm. An old man on a stone bench, waiting beside an ornamental well for birds to return to come summer, wrapped in multi-scarved winter and brown galoshes. He said, 'Tom and Viv attended my father's funeral in Eastbourne. Charles Haigh-Wood was buried in bright sunshine on a boiling day. Viv always described Tom that day. He stood looking down at the ditch. She said it was cold and black. But all around the day boiled. Tom had to stand back. He was sweating like a pig. Some sort of terror. Something about heat and cold. And this dark trench they'd dug for Dad. She said he never forgot that moment.' Maurice had a family perspective about his famous brother-in-law, and remarked of previous scholars who'd chased him up: 'They always came and asked me about Tom. They never once really asked me about Vivie, or Dad, or Mother, never asked me about the family. I'm quite interesting, too. After all, I'm the only broker known to history who lost half his fortune investing in Slater, Walker, in the middle of the property boom ... I mean, my God, my fingers were burned.'

Over these months, I realized I was being allowed a unique portrait of an Edwardian family, a family which had settled into genteel decay after the First War; and at one point I asked him why did he want to talk now, while he freely admitted he anticipated the fluttering wing of death? He said, 'It was only when I saw Vivie in the asylum for the last time I realized I had done something very wrong. She was as sane as I was. She said, 'God knows that may not amount to much, Maurice, but I'm as sane as you are,' and I did what I hadn't done for years. I sat in front of Vivie and actually burst into tears. No explanation. No good reason for it. Grown man and all. What Tom and I did was wrong. And Mother. I did everything Tom told me to. Not

'Here is a cartoon Viv did of me. I am battling my way through the Dardanelles. Her tremendous sense of fun. I called her Saigie. We had a standing joke between us about the war. She never quite understood how I survived. Great chums going down like flies. Towards the end of the war I located Padua; and much to the surprise of Colonel Verey, H.Q. 2nd Manchesters, I was still active. Then was struck low with trench fever and wheeled away to Bordighera. Just as I was recovering, I caught a dose of Spanish flu; lethal stuff, said to have caused more deaths in Italy than all the fighting. Colonel Verey was eager to get me back in the forward area. Alas, the Austrian–Italian armistice was declared October 1918. Bathed all afternoon in a river. Went to a Grand Ball at Val Salice, and met this little blonde, Contessina Tea di Gropello. Afterwards, she and I sent each other picture postcards for two years before it fizzled out. Viv used to ask me how on earth I survived the war. I always replied, "Every bullet missed."'

– Maurice Haigh-Wood

ashamed to say so. But when it came to our family, I think he bit off more than he could chew. He didn't understand the rules, actually. You see – you have to be kind to Vivie.'

The Colonel's one love, his wife, Ahmé Hoagland, an American cabaret dancer, had gone before him. The pair had planned a new villa in Portugal. And Maurice had blithely ordered the villa from London. It – or most of it – was built to their absentee specification. In London, Ahmé was diagnosed for terminal cancer, and the Colonel's world collapsed about him. As for the villa – it had the familiar Haigh-Wood fate. Somehow the builders hadn't quite done their job. Awful discovery that the roof was not put on during the winter months. Ghastly tale about sewage pipes which did not reach beyond the garden gate. As for the swimming-pool . . .

Maurice and Ahmé had one child, 'Raggie'. The boy was Tom Eliot's godson. Raggie grew up being shunted from one third-rate public school to the next. He hardly ever saw his parents. There was the occasional sight of the hired car turning up at half-term, otherwise the boy was sadly alone. Raggie married a sweet and gentle girl called Mildred, had two daughters, and tragically killed himself.

After Ahmé died, and what was left of that villa sold off at some loss, the Colonel had come to the end of his days, packed up his partnership in the stockbroker firm, gave up his room at the Onslow Court Hotel, sold up the odd property he had elsewhere, and was now cornered in a stuffy room beside this playwright chap who had a hundred questions. Whilst a vigilant housekeeper kept adding water to the gin on the side-table, with not a Craven 'A' in sight, and a four-to-five-on tip for the 2.30 at Doncaster was hardly a bet he should waste his bookmaker's time with, life had become thin and hardly worth going on with. But he did want to talk. Some of the past appeared guilty. There was a certain openness of spirit, perhaps recognized in Edmund Husserl's dismissal of despair: 'Negation cancels, affirmation underlines.' The Colonel was prepared to speak.

My research opened up some new avenues. I managed to track down the matron of the asylum where Viv died; attempted

TELEPHONE,
PADDINGTON 3331.

9, CLARENCE GATE GARDENS,

N. W. 1.

October 13, 1921

Dear Scofield

Tom has had rather a serious breakdown, & has had to stop all work, & go away for 3 months. He has broken a strict regimen, & now only read (for pleasure, not profit) 2 hours a day. Before he went, he fortunately secured St. John Hutchinson to do the London letter for the Dial. I have just written to Mr. Seldes to tell him, & also to say that—

Letter from Vivienne to Scofield Thayer, 1921: 'Tom has had rather a serious breakdown ...'

to unlock a unique friendship Viv formed with a chemist, Louise Purdon, which stretched over twenty-five years; and there were friends and relatives of doctors who had attended Vivienne Eliot.

A week or so before *Tom and Viv* opened in February 1984, at the Royal Court Theatre, there was a slight 'flutter of the dovecotes of literary London'. Before the actors got a chance to set foot on the stage, there came a warning bolt. The poet Sir Stephen Spender flew into the printed air with the dignity of a fluffy-footed bantam suddenly savaged by a polecat. He announced: 'This play is implausible, unpleasant, and of absolutely no substance.' As he hadn't seen the play or read it, this was an utterance chiefly to be praised for its extrasensory perception. Not a moment later, a hasty letter appeared in *The Times Literary Supplement* from L. C. Knights, who declared: 'I do not think I shall be drawn to see the play' and went on to insinuate that *Tom and Viv* was not far removed from 'prurient delight' in an 'abounding gutter'. As it happened, the play opened to exceptionally generous notices from the somewhat nervous critics who, like myself, were not entirely certain what kind of theatrical fiction had been let loose. There were a few dissenting voices. Humphrey Carpenter, who reviewed the play on radio, did not think too kindly of the interpretation of Tom Eliot, and he quoted sections from his private copy of Mary Trevelyan's diary to illustrate where I had gone wrong. This very diary he'd denied me access to. Later, he justified this behaviour by declaring he'd never had the slightest wish I should be allowed to 'pick the plums' which he'd inherited. And a journalist for the *London Review of Books* found himself so incensed by the play he could not contain himself. In such a hurry was he to turn out his article that he was unable to sit through the second half of *Tom and Viv*. He found the play 'a thin, staccato pageant that aims to win applause', and was equally unhappy with the play's audience: 'In addition there are the audience's O-level guffaws to contend with.' Shortly after, Helen Gardner made an announcement: 'Even if the play had been less awful from this and other reviews, it is outrageous that a great writer, barely twenty years dead, should be impersonated by an actor on the stage.' But why this anger from people who had scarcely bothered to see the play? After all, there is a fairly identifiable tradition in theatre of plays which characterize the famous – from Aristophanes on Cleon, to Brecht on Hitler, to Brenton on Churchill, or to Griffiths on Gramsci. If these plays of personal heresy were to be dismissed, it would mean casting off whole sections of over two thousand four hundred years of stage writing.

In due course, a column in *The New York Times*, written by Christopher Ricks, attempted to put an end to all this nonsense. He came running to the rescue of any clairvoyant who hated *Tom and Viv* but hadn't actually seen it. According to Ricks there is a perfect get-out clause. Ricks declared there is a 'great remark by F. R. Leavis' which makes theatre trips to the Royal Court virtually irrelevant. Evidently, Leavis was once asked if he'd read a book whose author he deplored. Leavis's reply was: 'To read it would be to condone it.' Now, is this the advent of the New Gosses of the barbarian hour? Or is there a distinct Bunterish howl from the cupboard of mortarboards? I say, yaroo, chaps, it's that bounder Stinkie Yoicks from over the Council Estate with his eggfarts. Lock the dorm. Close the Club membership. Under the floorboards, chaps [*wheeze*], until he's gone. And hide the jelly babies.

I assume this animus from certain quarters does not arise out of a wish to conceal, but that these imputations of foul motive and impenitent vulgarity are to protect Eliot; but when prejudgements defy reason they become the irrational cries from what might be termed mandarins of academic paraquat. There may indeed be more varmints and scalliwag cowboys in the litcrit penswill than in the combined ranks of the London Metropolitan Police, but what good does this do for Eliot? What has happened to this unique poet, who spoke of the man who suffers and the mind which creates? Where is the life of this poet whose own autobiography is no more than the remark: 'My life has been a Dostoevsky novel written by Middleton Murry'? What of the St Louis boy who read Savonarola years before Huck Finn? Or the emigrant poet who eschewed Carlos Williams's cadences of breath, and instead opted for cockneyisms (and cod as Coward) in a foreign street dialect? Or this scissored resolve to detach personality – a circumcision of the heart? Little help is provided by the understanding that no official biography will be allowed, or that there are a thousand Eliot letters sequestrated in Princeton University until 2020. And yet the Eliot estate and Faber & Faber appear to have formed a chums' club of clams around the man and his work. Meanwhile, an extraordinary number of pornographic verses, poems in many drafts, numerous letters and associative material are quietly exchanged in photostatted secretiveness amongst a select few. And, of course, none of this would be of any importance but for the fact that perhaps no posthumous career of a public figure in modern letters has been handled with such provoking obstructiveness since Isabel Burton set light to Dirty Dick's literary whiskers in 1890.

Why such animus over a play? In particular a play about Eliot? Is it because the very presence of an actor impersonating the poet drives something of a coach and horses through the theory of impersonality, and the belief in the artist's need for an extinction of his personality? But what other way is there to debate Eliot on the stage? The answer to this problem may lie in Husserl's view of personality. Far from being a mirror which only reflects surfaces (Eliot), personality may be a constituent of experience from which it is not possible to unhinge oneself. In Husserl's terms, a husband who denies himself the love of a woman in exchange for a devotion elsewhere is creating a pattern of behaviouristic perversion. The larger nature of the man is reduced, there is a limiting of the natural standpoint Husserl indicates, and though 'the wakeful life of our personality is a continuous perceiving actual or potential', such a man can only diminish his being. Transcendental knowledge, even that gained through the everyday momentum of personality, remains knowledge gained within experience. And the possibility arises that Eliot took a fundamentally mechanistic view of personality as something base and soiled which had to be detached. In so doing he approached Belief with the curious notion, during the early twenties, that a man only needs to be jolted by any trivial series of events to achieve a Faith. At the culmination of this

journey, he gave himself up to the Anglo-Catholic church with
the grace of passionate surrender. No matter the cost to his
personal life. Or, for that matter, any explanation to those who
were under the impression that the poet of *Prufrock* and *The
Waste Land* was a revolutionary artist, an inventor of form, and
a public spokesman for the notion of a fragmented world.
Instead, the man acquired Classicism, entertained the idea of
Royalty in an ideal society, was baptized in the Church of
England and took up British nationality. His critics from the
Republican Left, particularly those American friends out in the
cold now, accused him of taking an antinomian pathway to an
aloof, locked kingdom filled with sexual disgust and human
withdrawal. Others, like Wyndham Lewis, articulated that Eliot
was hiding 'in a volatilized hypostasization of his personal
feelings'. Whatever that may mean.

Eliot was not alone in appearing to represent the artist with
a revolutionary form. In music, Charles Ives in the States had
begun to break up the symphonic mould with cacophonic intru-
sions of trivial scraps, street sounds and band parades. Nevertheless, these achievements were made in musical isolation, and the
fragments of symphonic language maintained some linear con-
formity. Ives's musical pictures were strictly within a narrative
context. But the painter Kurt Schwitters, by elevating frottage
to the art of disintegrated vision, was the nearest equivalent to
Eliot. In those times, Ezra Pound could be relied upon to sum-
marize the aim of the artist: 'Make it new.' But the suspicion
remains, these artists were as much devoted to the idea of
novelty as they were to an intrinsic nausea for a scratched and
overworked cultural field. In retrospect it does not appear so
surprising that the revolutionary stylist turns out to be an apolo-
gist for High Church and ruling-class loyalty. Ernst Fischer found
nothing strange in a bourgeois society when 'stylized art is
bound up with aristocratic systems and realist art with working-
class movements'; it could well be that those who shared the first
joy on publication of *The Waste Land* were somewhat misled.
There was an apprehension of the 'new' in form. But when they
investigated the content, were these recognitions of despair just

a pleasurable exchange of new decencies being observed? A shift of taste and judgement, nothing more. Fischer indicates: 'Form is the manifestation of the state of equilibrium ... We might define form as conservative and content as revolutionary.'

But the greatness of the early Eliot cannot be separated from the accidental form of his poetry. The poetry appears to link with the exact waywardness of the modern mind. Broken phrases, torn moments, derelict street echoes on the edge of the ear, the tissue and shard of glimpsed reveries. D. S. Mirsky, a rather undervalued Eliot critic, attempted one of the earliest definitions: 'What distinguishes Eliot is that with him a rare poetic gift is allied with a social theme of real significance, his contemporaries are but manifestations of the death of bourgeois poetry and civilization; he alone has been able to create a poetry of this death.'

Perhaps no poet since Wordsworth has written such perfect fragments:

The boat responded
Gaily, to the hand expert with sail and oar
The sea was calm, your heart would have responded
Gaily, when invited, beating obedient
To controlling hands

beside so much dross:

On the Rialto once,
The rats are underneath the piles.
The Jew is underneath the lot.
Money in furs. The boatman smiles.

and still be so keen elsewhere to commit the odd Semite to a further dose of water and slime:

Your Bleistein lies
Under the flatfish and the squids.
Graves' Disease in a dead Jew's eyes!
When the crabs have eat the lids.
Lower than the wharf rats dive.

Is there no break at all for the fish-snuffed Jews?

From the early years, Eliot's apparent bourgeois horror was not confined to race: in April 1921 he wrote to Richard Aldington. He described his profound hatred for democracy, a continuous physical horror, a horror to be sane in the midst of all this, it was too dreadful, too huge and 'It goes too far for rage.' This naked disgust exhibited itself elsewhere. Eliot replied to a friend's letter of fulsome praise; he simply enclosed a cutting from the *Midwives' Record* and underlined the words 'blood', 'mucus', 'shreds of mucus', 'purulent offensive discharge'. (The first letter not so much the student of F. H. Bradley, more shades of Johan Huizinga; the second letter less Laforgue, more the sexual revulsion of Otto Weininger.) So small wonder is it that many a critic from the Left has weighed in heavily. Cries of 'reactionary' and 'sterile' art. Imprecations that the work is anti-human and life-hating. And further noises off from *Soviet Literature Today* about the necessity to be a puppet of decadence to appreciate Eliot's poetry. Not to be outdone by *Spearhead*, the organ of the British Fascist Party, which calmly announced that T. S. Eliot was their 'Great British Racialist' for the July 1982 edition. According to *Spearhead*: 'His masterpiece *The Waste Land* represents this civilization as a thing of barren materialism pulled up by its race-cultural roots.' And it quoted Eliot with cavalier charm: 'It may be argued that complete equality means universal irresponsibility.'

In more recent times, Eliot's overt anti-semitism has taken on a less comic quality. The 45-year-old poet who visited the University of Virginia in 1933 and lectured on why 'reasons of race and religion combine to make any large number of free-thinking Jews undesirable' can barely be excused his remarks. Those protectors who ran forward to claim it was a common jollity of the time to slag yids have a certain ugly thinness. Here was a highly respected figure at a campus in the southern states which itself appeared to endorse a policy of student apartheid. And in National Socialist Germany, months before Eliot reached Virginia, the ruling National Socialistische Deutsche Arbeiter Partei passed a Law for the Restoration of the Professional Civil Service which, in effect, forbade all 'non-Aryans' access to senior teaching-posts. By the time Eliot reached Virginia, the Reich Chamber of Culture was insisting on an elaborate genealogical questionnaire for every professor of literature in Germany. Such shockwaves across the academic ocean were scarcely unheard even in Virginia.

So this public figure and his pronouncements fitted uncomfortably beside the dazzling achievement of the poetry. This Anglican and Royalist was to be found pronouncing on his preference for fascism and, further, that his fundamental objection to fascism was merely that it appeared pagan. In due course, this respected poet acquired a carelessness of public utterance – phrases abounded along the lines that only a small number of people living have achieved the right not to be a communist. He also noted that the great majority of human beings should go on living in the place in which they were born. Far from stating the obvious here, wasn't it Eliot himself who'd become a naturalized British citizen? The general air of pontification reached a pitch when he paid homage to the ideal that family is the root of all culture. It took little insight from his friends to register that Eliot endured an appallingly painful marriage for seventeen years with Vivienne Haigh-Wood, that they both underwent an exacting process of legal separation, and that for the last decade of her life she remained in a North London asylum not six miles away from his office at Faber & Faber. Cracks in the public face had a very private edge about them.

The public face naturally included the poetry. And here Eliot most carefully nurtured a protective coating around the work. As far as he was concerned the progress of an artist is the continual extinction of personality. The key passages come from his essay 'Tradition and the Individual Talent'. Eliot wrote: 'What happens is a continual surrender of himself as he is at the moment to something which is more valuable. The progress of an artist is a continual self-sacrifice, a continual extinction of personality.' It has been taken that Eliot here postulates that what is going on inside the poem is of greater significance than the artist's personality. A further passage, however, indicates that the artist may not entirely be in control of his own material. Eliot wrote:

'There is a great deal in the writing of poetry which must be conscious and deliberate. In fact, the bad poet is usually unconscious where he ought to be conscious, and conscious where he ought to be unconscious. Both errors tend to make him "personal". Poetry is not a turning loose of a emotion, but an escape from emotion; it is not the expression of personality but an escape from personality.' Yet to find value in the work which transcends personality is not quite the same thing as finding in poetry a harbour in which to escape from emotion. His decidedly restive tone is curious. A discrepancy strains in among these passages. It cannot be wholly inappropriate to ask of the artist in Eliot – an escapee from what emotion? Eliot did once describe a place of paranoid delusion where the outside is seen as true hell: 'In a world of fugitives the person taking the opposite direction will appear to run away.' He paints a surreal landscape. Escape may seem like a man climbing a downward escalator. He doesn't move at all. A state of being not a mile away from what Pound called Eliot's 'Possum position', a creature which remains motionless when threatened. Thus, it is pertinent to note these passages which became foundation stones of New Criticism. But recognitions have emerged that much of his early work came out of the pain within the marriage, and far from being a catalogue of a fragmented culture, *The Waste Land* is a more personal but indirect form of literary autobiography. And Viv, that painted shadow in the background, somewhat Stalinized into cultural obscurity, may have been something a little less than his muse but much more than the pitiful wraith supposedly hung round his neck like a bag of ferrets. Rebecca West wrote: 'He never stopped writing about Vivienne until *The Confidential Clerk*, and that was 1953.'

In the main, it is difficult to see quite how Viv can be ignored for Tom met her in Oxford, 1914. Six months later they were married in a London registry office. She was known as Viv or Vivienne. She was a mimic and a dancer, with a talent for poetry and watercolours, a vivacious woman from a well-connected family who introduced Eliot to British music halls and ballet. They shared an interest in cats and French language and espoused mutual love for identical books (*Daphnis and Chloe* and Chateaubriand's Indian love affair set against a voyage up the Mississippi, *Atala*). Eliot declared: 'I find her still perpetually baffling and deceptive, she seems to me like a child of six with an immensely clever and precocious mind ... and I can never escape from the spell of her persuasive (even coercive) gift of argument.' It is Eliot, again, in the early twenties to Ellen Thayer, who wrote a description of one of Viv's stories: 'It seems to me amazingly brilliant and humorous and horrible, and I have never read anything in the least like it. It is likely to attract a great deal of notice here.' (The story is 'The Paralysed Woman'.)

But it is necessary to distinguish between the simple presence of someone who inhabits the world of unwashed coffee cups and the domestic brawls which ensue over vanished lavatory rolls, and the working partner who shares, and indeed occupies, the day alongside one. For example – Viv is writing to Scofield Thayer from London, and she says that Tom has had to take a holiday. There is a bittersweet intimacy in her words. For she and Thayer were lovers before Tom found either of them at Oxford. 'I believe you invited me to come and drown myself with you once. I am ready at any moment. Tom says – delighted to review Joyce. That at least is definite. Will let you know if anything happens to or with Lady Rothermere, not that you will have any interest. Yours, V.'

Thayer, owner and editor of the *Dial* magazine, in America, received another letter from Viv, dated October 1921. This time of a more serious nature. Viv was left in order to cope, and Tom had departed to be very ill indeed.

Dear Scofield

Tom has had rather a serious breakdown, & has had to stop all work, & go away for 3 months. He has to follow a strict regimen, and may only read (for pleasure, not profit) 2 hours a day. Before he went he fortunately secured St John Hutchinson to do the London Letter for the *Dial*. I have just written to Mr Seldes to tell him, & also to say that ...

Do you want to wait until February for the review of Marianne

Moore's poems? If so, Tom could do it for you in January and would like to. I forgot to mention this to Mr Seldes, so now I suppose I shall have to write again. Unless you will — you have nothing to do I presume, and look at *my* position.

I have not nearly finished my own nervous breakdown yet. Tom is going to be in England for about a month from now, (he is at Margate), and then will be able to go and occupy Lady Rothermere's villa at La Tourbie.

By this you will see that Tom and Lady Rothermere have clicked. A Quarterly has been arranged between them which Tom was to edit in his spare time, and to get what pickings he could from the inadequate sum laid down by her in the name of literature. Everything is now postponed until January.

Towards the end of November *I want* to go somewhere. I don't know yet, and it does not much matter, but I must escape from England or it will smother me. Have been trying to escape for 5–6 years!

I do expect you to come to London in the Spring, or perhaps before. Meanwhile I may appear in Vienna.

Viv.

Certainly, on the surface it appears it is the companion who can cope. A few days later, she is writing to Violet Schiff: 'I have been so anxious to know how you were. I have tried to write each day, but have had so many letters to do for Tom.' But has this companion become also a working partner? Viv wrote to Sydney Schiff shortly after the publication of *The Waste Land*: 'I want to thank you on my account for showing such real and true appreciation of *The Waste Land*. Perhaps not even you can entirely know with what emotion I saw *The Waste Land* go out into the world. It means to me a great deal of what you have described and it has become a part of me (or I of it) this last year.'

Is this the same 'bag of ferrets' Virginia Woolf pulled out of her Bloomsbury insult book? Do we recognize the 'awful wraith who *drinks* ether' according to the 'medicinal authority' of Aldous Huxley? But, yet, within fifteen years, Tom would be writing to a friend that he believes she will flourish better without him, and he has resolved never to see her again, and that he didn't believe it was any good for a woman to live with a man to whom she is morally, in the larger sense, unpleasant, as well as physically indifferent.

A paradox emerges. When we look at Viv a shaking, dependent Tom steps forth. When we glimpse at what there is of their work together in manuscript, an eager, positive Viv, literate but impulsive, trips across the page.

There is a tentative hint that perhaps there was much more to bittersweet breakdowns and financial despair, and Tom and Viv found at times a sensible working relationship. She may not simply have been the muse, filling thirty-three years with remorse and anguish, she indeed exchanged with him his fragments, and offered her own broken talents and fragile cries at the streaming centre of their life together. And it is by looking at her that we can more assuredly grasp the highly wrought nerved-stroke of their partnership. But this look also requires a certain leap into the dark stillness of the past, and a degree of caution; it is too early to place Viv in a position of being more than the Cynthia of Propertius, and at the same time less than Camille Claudel of Rodin's studio (who it seems made three classic mistakes in life – she married the artist, sculpted 'The Kiss' for him, and was then obliged to spend the rest of her life in an asylum). I do not assume a radical feminist is going to prove that Viv wrote *The Waste Land*, but it remains now a task for any dabbler in Eliotian metaphysics to demonstrate that he could have written it without her.

The interweaving of the material is the clue. We are hearing a familiar voice in an excised section of *The Waste Land*. Curiously, the names repeat themselves. In due course they become cross-referenced with a poem not by Tom but by Viv, thus 'Fresca'.

'Gerontion' was written during the first half of 1919. The last ten lines invite an image of domestic and private words, intimacies of diary notes, cats, names perhaps, a neighbour's title above a doorbell:

What will the spider do?
Suspend its operations, will the weevil
Delay? De Bailhache, Fresca, Mrs Cammel, whirled

Beyond the circuit of the shuddering Bear
In fractured atoms.

'The Fire Sermon' (Part III: *The Waste Land*), completed in the
later months of 1921, was subject to near brutal editing by Ezra
Pound. Such was the Caesarean operation, seventy or so opening lines were excised. This section indicates a languorous cat
named Fresca who 'yawns and gapes, and dreams of love and
pleasant rapes', scribbles verse of a gloomy nature; and this
'prudent, sly, domestic puss puss cat' makes an arrival suggesting
nine lives, echo of nine goddesses. Pound had had enough of
gossipy Fresca, her sexual life, a doorstep dunged by every dog
in town; and though Viv made efforts to retrieve lines, Pound
returned the section to its principal image of rat-scuttling
London life, the tragedy of Tiresias's ambiguous sexual unease,
and immolation of a sermon preached by the Buddha tearing at
the gross belly of lust − 'The Fire Sermon'. But a few of these
chipped-away lines have a Viv-like resonance:

My dear, how are you? I'm unwell today,
And have been, since I saw you at the play.
I hope that nothing mars your gaiety,
And things go better with you, than with me.
I went last night − more out of dull despair −
To Lady Kleinwurm's party − who was there
Oh, Lady Kleinwurm's monde − no one that mattered.
Somebody sang, and Lady Kleinwurm chattered.
What are you reading? Anything that's new?
I have a clever book by Giraudoux.

In 1924 Viv contributed her second 'Letters of the Moment'
to the *Criterion* magazine, under the initials F.M. She made quick
and passing reference to the idea of 'The Fire Sermon'; she wrote:
'I once performed an act of self-immolation by attending a
birthday-party dance at Hampstead.' Her article specifically re-
built lines of a poem which she represented with a certain
proprietorial skill. She included these lines:

When sniffing Chloe, with the toast and tea,
Drags back the curtains to disclose the day,

The amorous Fresca stretches, yawns and gapes,
Aroused from dreams of love in curious shapes.
The quill lies ready at her finger tips;
She drinks, and pens a letter while she sips;
'I'm very well, my dear, and how are you?
I have another book by Giraudoux.'

Now, the original version of 'The Fire Sermon' had been cut down by Pound. The opening twenty lines became four lines. And these were mashed at a later stage:

Admonished by the sun's inclining ray,
White-armed Fresca blinks, and yawns, and gapes.
Her hands caress the egg's well-rounded dome,
She sinks in revery, till the letters come.

But in Viv's 'Letters of the Moment' (1924) she cannot resist claiming these lines back. She includes them, thus:

Her hands caress the egg's well-rounded dome;
As her mind labours till the phrases come.

There is a hint of admonishment. A gentle reminder that she will rework what she once possessed. Harry Levin, the author of a pioneering study of Joyce, indicated Viv's voice might be registered in more of the work. Levin remarked that Viv had a tone which permeated, and the woman who contributed: 'What have you got married for if you don't want to have children' and 'If you don't like it you can get on with it' has the similar poignant cry, burned-out shrill nerve-ends and ashen sheets laid waste with empty arms: 'My nerves are bad tonight. Yes, bad. Stay with me ...'

The publication of the text of Eliot's 'Sweeney Agonistes' occurred during the final physical separation between Tom and Viv. Eliot borrows from St John of the Cross, and places these words before the poem: 'Hence the soul cannot be possessed of the divine union, until it has divested itself of the love of created beings.' A couple of months after this, Tom instructed his solicitors to prepare a deed of separation from Vivienne. The following three years became an unreal and paranoid existence for them both. Tom retreated to corners, friends' homes, hotel rooms, the barricades of Faber & Faber, and the discreet silence of his associates. Meanwhile, Viv, unable to as much as speak to him on the phone, having her panic-struck letters returned to her by a Faber office boy, knowing each mutual friend she and Tom possessed would blatantly lie, began a descent into a pitiable condition. Cultural teddybears were gathering for a misogynists' picnic. The more Viv struck out in dismay, through eccentricities and erratic desire to draw attention, the more insistent the murmurs about the inexpiable harridan.

It was what was done to her in Tom's name which hurt the most. And his associates and allies tended to overreact. Viv's diary records an incident when Louise Purdon stayed overnight with her. At dawn five bailiffs broke down the front door and removed books and paintings along with some Haigh-Wood silverware. The women were shaken and terrified. Two days later, Viv had to write to Geoffrey Faber, at the publishers, to ask for the return of her own books, her family silver and a complete set of the *Criterion*. To his credit, Faber promptly complied.

Since 1911 Eliot had maintained a regular correspondence with Emily Hale in Cambridge, Massachusetts. During these years there were indications that the ever-patient Emily harboured a belief she might one day marry Tom. And between 1932 and 1937 – the most acute period of Viv's despair – Emily Hale's holiday visits to see Tom gained frequency. They regularly visited friends in the country. They were recognized very much as a couple together. No matter the upright depth of honesty of this friendship, it was behaviour on Eliot's part nudging cruelty, for Viv knew. And her fevered imagination feared the worst.

In the mid-thirties such was Viv's ostracism she could barely sink lower. She wrote out a small cheque to Eliot personally. Posted it to Faber & Faber, with a note, asking for a recent publication. She haunted her bank until the manager was able to confirm that the cheque had actually been cashed. The simple pleasure of getting that cheque back was enough for her. At least he did exist somewhere in London. He had passed the cheque through his own account. The relief in her mind, that finally something she had done was acknowledged by him. The critic Bonamy Dobrée remonstrated with Eliot over the words in the front of 'Sweeney Agonistes'; Eliot replied: 'Merely to kill one's human affection will get one nowhere, it would be only to become rather more a completely living corpse than most people are. But the doctrine is fundamentally true.'

It reached a point at the portals of Faber & Faber. Viv was now barred from entering the building. In her determined way, she made a habit of popping bars of his favourite chocolate into the letter-box. On one chocolate-visiting-day she pushed too hard at the door. There was an unseemly altercation in the hall. Shouts were heard. Tom's secretary, Bridget O'Donovan, hurried downstairs to calm Viv, and to reassure her that he was not in the building. This ploy enabled Eliot to slip out a back way. It comes as no surprise to learn this hardly placated the poor woman. Viv knew when she was being lied to. It remains something of a greater surprise to conjure up a vision of the man reaching for his brolly, bowler and spats, and hurling himself, it seems, down the Faber fire-escape with all the abandon of Harold Lloyd.

O'Donovan has written a memoir of her years as Eliot's secretary. And she was led to believe, like many others, that Viv was 'schizophrenic', and that that was the medical finding which caused her to be put into the asylum. But, at the time, there was no legal requirement whatsoever to commit a person on grounds of schizophrenia. Her doctors were only obliged to show 'she is an individual, no longer able to fulfil her duty because of unsoundness of mind, and is therefore a fit and proper person to be detained', under the Government Reception Order, Section 4, 1890 Lunacy Act. Grotesque as this may sound, there was no alternative definition of state of being which would satisfy the Lower Court. In private, Eliot expressed his own misgivings about her various doctors; above all, if she had been suffering from schizophrenia alone, Eliot and her brother Maurice would assuredly have found for Viv the proper treatment which even then was available. Her doctors, Cyriax, Treves, Moore, Miller and Balmer, confined themselves to a primitive round of suppressants and bromides, such that by the late thirties her body could no longer take the alcohol-based compounds, hence the acute swellings of wrists and ankles and glands, and her own chronic aversion to social imbibing. 'Please make it clear,' said Maurice, 'Viv never touched alcohol.' Of course she didn't, she was saturated with medicinal alcohol until she reached the confines of Northumberland House.

Viv did not possess a Leonard Woolf in her life. For Woolf on several occasions put Virginia into homes and signed her in and out on 'forty-day reception orders'. Ultimately, both Tom and Maurice settled for the opinions of her doctors. It may appear ludicrous in the present day to hear of intelligent men swallowing the punitive prescriptions which were handed out, but it is not an easy matter to apportion any blame. Nor for that matter is it necessary. For both Tom and Maurice were very much figures of their time; it was Viv who was seen constantly as 'the problem', and the social mores of the family tribe provided a suitable solution. The Haigh-Wood family learned from expensive medical opinion that madness was an inherited disease; in addition, they and their pliant American son-in-law found themselves caught in a web of social taboo. Rose Haigh-Wood preferred to call it 'moral insanity', a phrase with a ring of authority about it, suitable to apply to a person who was unable to fulfil her duty in life. What is perhaps more disturbing is the social machinery to this end. The ramifications of Viv's internment really did not finish at the gates of the asylum. There was her own money to clear up. Her property. Her books. Her clothes and jewellery. And the deep regret and remorse which clung to both men over this matter. And also the very serious problem which arises from internment. For Viv had no legal right to appeal against her condition, now made all the more distressing by the fact that no apparent attempt was ever made to secure her release. Private asylums like Northumberland House were run on somewhat self-serving lines. The wealthier inmates such as Viv were not encouraged to leave. It always came back to the doctors.

I had made an earlier note about Dr Reginald Miller's reference to a certain 'moral barometer' during the course of my research. During the rehearsal period a senior psychologist visited the Company and identified these words as a Grundyism. The 'moral barometer' purports to measure high points of oestrus during menstruation. Years before Viv was put inside, the social requirements of the time were so inhibiting that her doctors found it fitting to put all aspects of menstrual irregularity down to 'female illness'. And in her early teens Viv was brought up to believe that she was to blame. It resulted in a chronic obsession to send home all sheets from school to be washed, and there were instances when she stayed at friends or put up in hotels, and she invariably took the bedlinen back to the Haigh-Wood servants to have it washed. It is ultimately ironic that the asylum, which was not disposed to alcohol-based compounds, therefore provided a harbour of calm after the years of punitive diagnoses. And perhaps it is instructive to note that, according to her brother, Viv acquired a serenity after menopause which enabled her to take up her short stories and her watercolour painting, and her dancing.

Tom and Maurice had no other choice but to believe those particular doctors. What else was there to believe? Eliot wrote: 'It is better to be stupid in faith, even in a stupid faith, than to be stupid and believe nothing.' They were partners inside the family net, tenants-in-common to an Edwardian estate in a dry land; afterwards, both men shared anguish, there was a nerved tremor in the mind of recall, succubus of regret, the painted shadow turned into wraith would not go away, and Viv floated in on their shores of memory.

It was these very hauntings and echoes of remorse which, during the writing of *Tom and Viv*, led me to realize this was not entirely the realm of the biographer. Nor was it the stuff of the documentary play. But what is this kind of writing? In earlier plays about Lee Harvey Oswald, or Saint-Just, or Amin, I kept to an Aristophanic mould. It was after reading Herman Broch's *The Death of Virgil* that I realized a form had emerged which, for want of a better term, might be called critical fiction. But one might well cavil that the Broch is a work of a novelist. Yet what kind of a novel is it which subsumes more than a hundred pages of Virgil in the text? In the marketplace, where the biography appears to have poached many of the fiction writer's tools, some of this equipment ought to be returned to the imaginative writer. By this I mean it is wholly doubtful that a study to the point of exhaustiveness of Henry James can lead one back to the novelist; but a work such as *The Death of Virgil* might well return the reader back to a most profound interpretation of *The Aeneid*. It may not be necessary to press the point that here in Hermann Broch is a novelist using his fiction in the form of a critique. I'd like to suggest that the umbrella of critical fiction can be extended also in other fields. In the auditorium, Bartók's 'Concerto for Orchestra' makes analysis of the politics of certain sections of Shostakovich's 'Leningrad Symphony'. And in painting, Velasquez's 'Las Meninas' is adopted by Manet's social appetite, and ultimately debauched by Picasso's optical verve in the Cubist mould. If there is a major flaw in the notion of critical fiction it is that such writing perhaps expects too much of the ordinary hardworking professional critic. I mean by this that it's not so easy for a critic to produce a comment on Milton in the form of a poem the equal of his subject (perchance – an honourable exception – Samuel Johnson's *Comus: New Prologue*).

My intention here has been to indicate that critical fiction might extend the writer to areas which would normally be lost to the biographer; while working on *Tom and Viv* I found this overriding pall of a past buried with guilt but this could not be easily translated into narrative or documentation. And when I suggest that the past has to be regained, I mean that we have been thrown up various pictures of men and women, their work and happiness, but in too many cases shapes have not been fully drawn and certain figures are often only noticeable by their absence. And some quality of the past ought to be redeemed. A measure of what it was. A flash of happiness between a man and a woman no record of the years can hope to illuminate. I can appreciate Walter Benjamin's desire to take back, even change, our view of the past:

Reflection shows us that our image of happiness is thoroughly coloured by the time to which the course of our own existence has assigned us. The kind of happiness that could arouse envy in us exists only in the air we have breathed, among people we could have talked to, women who could have given themselves to us. In other words, our image of happiness is indissolubly bound up with the image of redemption. The same applies to our view of the past, which is the concern of history. The past carries with it a temporal index by which it is referred to redemption.

Great love for each has something to do with giving back to the other a sense of wholeness; when a person has committed a crime in the past thrashing the dead can hardly help; but to return to the past a configuration of moment and place (as with a play) suggests a greater link, what perhaps Eliot meant by his 'present moment of the past'. The redeemed historicity.

When *Tom and Viv* began its preliminary run at the Royal Court Theatre, there was a vigorous response from letters, every day, by people who had seen the play. Lawrentians who were determined to file a claim for 'life as against art' in the play. Husbands with enslaved wives who were not too sure if I had ultimately let them off the hook. For the play's short run the theatre was packed to the gods, with even queues for the matinees. There were farmers who hadn't read a poem for years (agricultural fair at Earl's Court?) and Eliot students deep into a second year; working-class families side by side with the tang of pin-striped perfume from the carriage trade. A dishevelled figure loaded up with books entered the foyer carrying a ferret in a cage; he clutched a ticket for the show. But Anne Jenkins, the General Manager, had a wintry eye. 'What is that?' 'It's my ferret in a cage, may I put it in the cloaks?' 'You certainly may not.' 'I'll put it under my seat then.' 'No, sir, that ferret is not coming into my theatre.' 'What shall I do with it?' 'I suggest you take it across the Square and put your ferret in the gents' public loo,' replied the General Manager. An elderly gentleman sat in the centre of a long row jumped up several times to excuse himself during the play's performance. He was in an agitated state. He'd climbed over a dozen pairs of knees and back until a point of exasperation was reached. A salesperson in the foyer took his arm and he muttered gravely, 'I just can't help it, I so loathe this play, I can't sit still. I have to keep coming out.' The salesperson suggested politely, 'Why don't you just sit down, sir, in your seat and just enjoy a really good loathe?' She led him back down the aisle like a lamb. And a conservatively dressed woman in the front stalls had reached the part in the play when the character of Viv, as played, announces undying love for this man who has left her in an asylum for ten years. The woman leapt to her feet and called out, 'That proves it, she *was* schizophrenic!' And marched out of the theatre.

The theatre as such does not, I believe, hold many limitations. The theatrical scope is wide indeed, so long as the audience can be convinced by the artifice. The theatrical throw is fine – look here is essential character, now we are in a bedroom in Venice, here is a witty sleight of personality etc.; but it is what the play leaves in the audience's mind which has the greatest effect. On other occasions it is what the play appears to leave out which can cause distress:

Dear Mr Hastings

I attended your play the other night. And I want you to know that not for an instant did I recognize the same great religious poet who wrote *Four Quartets*. May I explain myself more fully? I fought for three years in North Africa against an enemy I believed to be the enemy. When I got home, I looked about me and was less convinced just who was the enemy. All my instincts are Conservative, but all my idealism firmly belongs in the Labour camp. On being demobbed, I agreed with the country's belief in a need to rationalize whatever sources the State could muster. I also believed – when I looked at the great waste – the broken cities – the empty fields – the sandbagged mansions and kids' hospitals without roofs – that the past could not be wiped away. Like many hundreds of others, I discovered on reading *Four Quartets* a sense of release. It wasn't the Eliot of the early years. Here was a form of writing which elevated my soul, until I yearned to achieve Eliot's own goal of 'a condition of great simplicity'. I daresay Mr Eliot most probably got his Nobel Prize because of that poem. It spoke to me, and hundreds of men and women like me, it spoke of 'dead patrols' and it gave prayer and solace to 'women who have seen their sons or husbands setting forth, and not returning'. Out of purification we will go on. I saw in your play warring cries between men and women, admittedly great pain and remorse, but not for an instant the spiritual voyage the later Eliot set me on.

Yours sincerely ...

Indeed, much of *Four Quartets* represents the culmination of a career. But the public artist here recruits some less rigorous notions alongside his spiritual quest. Certain incongruous elements are found tamped together to reinforce the transcendentalism. There are, for example, sections of disingenuous nationalism, albeit in a pastoral metre of singular beauty:

> So, while the light fails
> On a winter's afternoon, in a secluded chapel
> History is now and England.

And there is a frank admission by Eliot that he once considered three of the *Quartets* primarily as patriotic pieces. It is curious, this mix of the banal with a finer but unspecific sense of remorse. Certain threnody remains weightless, attenuated, as if all persona must be vacated. And we may not know whose is:

> the rending pain of re-enactment
> Of all that you have done, and been; the shame
> Of motives late revealed, and the awareness
> Of things ill done and done to others' harm
> Which once you took for exercise of virtue.
> When fools' approval stings, and honour stains.
> From wrong to wrong the exasperated spirit
> Proceeds, unless restored by that refining fire
> Where you must move in measure like a dancer.

Yet of the four sections, 'Burnt Norton' does portray more of the writer. The house and the rose-garden, sunlight and footfalls and dust, and the reverie for an earlier remembered cityscape:

> the torpid
> Driven on the wind that sweeps the gloomy hills of London.
> Hampstead and Clerkenwell, Camden and Putney,
> Highgate, Primrose and Ludgate.

conjure up a recognizable topography of Tom and Viv's early
years together. The precise problem with *Four Quartets* is that
it was written during a crucial time when Viv was alive and in
a sense still shared this city with him. But in 'East Coker' the poet
has tried to distance himself:

So here I am in the middle way, having had twenty years –
Twenty years largely wasted ...

And it is not easy to understand how these lines could so occupy
the poet with their consuming self-reflection, written as they
were during the Second World War when Viv was very much
alive and abandoned in that asylum. Grief is the song of tragedy,
but I may never understand quite how a poet can set about *Four
Quartets*, in which he evokes a surface pattern of transfiguration
and a struggle for spiritual values along with notions of timeless
patriotism, while the unacknowledged object of so much of this
grief sat out those same years in a padlocked white room near
the Finsbury by-pass.

Nobody in their right mind is going to expect a great writer
to be a great man; but here is an artist quintessentially devoted
to dramatizing his introspection and the unredeemed horror
of emotional pain wrought from an intimate life, and yet he
allows the nostalgia and nationalism to avert us from these
deeper instincts; the poet and critic Christopher Hampton writes
'We are aware of the inadequacies and defects of his response
to the complex issues of the living world, we are at the same
time poignantly aware of his dilemmas as a man who had had
his path chosen for him, and nowhere more intensely than in the
lucid embodiment of the quest for being and place, for reconcilia-
tion and redemption, that marks the achievement of the *Four
Quartets*.' These wartime sequences were almost the last of the
real poetry in the man; this very theatrical poet had achieved a
further method of disguising the private suffering behind a flow
of public and patriotic language. But these barricades of his
theory of impersonality had begun to look patchy; could it be
that this very theory itself was something of a 'modern heresy'?
The early genius which had vacated spiritual sensibility was now

a man in search of an intensity more buried in temporal guilt; he wrote to a friend: 'To do away with a sense of guilt is to do away with civilization.' It remains, however, something of a gnostic's sleight of hand to elevate unspecific remorse to a universal cry.

A further incident which indicated the strength of the response from the Royal Court audience came when a thickset woman under a wide hat and a flowing winter coat, brandishing an umbrella, stood impatiently one night at the Stage Door. She insisted on meeting the actor who played the character of Tom with such formidable and uncanny likeness, and eventually she found him: 'I don't want you to think this play is about anything as grand as literary pretensions and all that. Forget about that, I say. I don't care if this play is called *Bert and Deb* or *Dick and Sylv*. This play is about one woman who loved one man to the exclusion of all others. And I want you to know this. Goodnight.' And wide hat, and brolly, and flying cloak disappeared into the rainy darkness of Sloane Square.

Essentially, every line of dialogue in *Tom and Viv* remains true to the nature of events; but not every scene observes the literal procession of the calendar. Essential features indent surfaces with a critique of tragic marble. These are not photographs. If one could take a Kodak snap of the truth, then a celluloid dimension of absolutes would become a compulsory C.S.E. course. There are areas in the story it is impossible to enter. Mercifully, the mystery which surrounds Tom's fascination with Burghley Mansions, St Martin's Lane, does not come into the subject of this play. A play can raise questions, and often imply affirmative answers, and *Tom and Viv* puts forward the proposition amongst others that an Edwardian Eliot strongly identified with the *haute bourgeoisie* of the Haigh-Wood family he married into, but he misunderstood the conceit of their class; what looked on the surface like the fossil order was something far more corrupt. And as man and artist, far from being the first of the new, he begins to emerge rather as the last of the old. New bourgeois form was merely a prop to entrench a reactive process of culture. And there are reflections on the theme that the emotional fascist of the artistic temper made public utterances on behalf of private turmoil.

Towards the end of the run of the play at the Royal Court, a friendly mole from inside Faber & Faber informed me: 'The week your play opened there was an element of panic and dismay here. Meetings behind closed doors. Mention of seeking solicitors' advice. Followed by a sense of relief. As if at last a boil had been lanced. Then came a gradual realization that it wasn't such a bad thing after all. And the powers-that-be studied the sales chart with relish. And fresh air came in. It was decided to hasten on with the publication of Eliot's letters. It didn't matter that a thousand of his letters to Emily Hale were still under embargo in America. Whatever else you've achieved, you appear to have provided incentive and determination to go public with Eliot, warts and all. Knowing this lot here – no one will thank you for that. I had, of course, my own reservations about *Tom and Viv*. I went alone one night, and hoped nobody would see me from the office. I found myself in a mood not unlike Maurice Haigh-Wood when he broke down in front of Viv at the end. For reasons I cannot justify I found myself in tears all the way through the second act. Tears which I could not explain in a rational sense at all. I tried not to look around me, but I detected many men and women sat side by side in those little seats reflecting on what they had each done to the other over the years. Why does the past hurt so? I don't know the answer.'

His own past which Eliot reflected on was profoundly influenced by women – Charlotte, his mother; his childhood love, Emily Hale; Vivienne Haigh-Wood and Mary Trevelyan; and, in Vivienne's case, the years they had really did hurt, but out of them he produced his finest work. As his achievement grew Viv's diminished, yet for a considerable period neither one was able to do without the other. In Vivienne's case, in terms of her wealth and social expectation, she married this young American student never to contemplate divorce or separation. And she could not have anticipated the social abuse and character assassination which was to come her way. For Eliot, there came a time when some of this pain could be assuaged.

In January 1957, ten years after Viv's death, Eliot married his secretary, Valerie Fletcher. He was sixty-eight. And in 1965 Eliot died in London of complications following a number of years distressed by pulmonary emphysema. Throughout this second marriage, both partners found an intensity of love and devotion which surprised many of his associates. What appeared on the surface to be a nursing expedition in the last days of this famous poet became a unique and untiring accommodation of a deeply shared and selfless affection. Although there remains a residue of criticism directed towards the widow who has now become the sole trustee of the Eliot estate, this must not in any way obscure the undoubted happiness and love the poet discovered with her in his later years. If anything, the present trustee has worked diligently to the best of her view towards the goal of a proper editorial policy over the posthumous career; she may well have been wrongly advised to obstruct certain studies when there was little need to entail suspicion, but on other occasions has gone out of her way to provide access for more lapdog hermeneutics.

What is at stake now is the content of the poetry. If it is the music of an age, it remains an equivocal distinction to find the music unimpeachable but the age as something less; even the artist who stands vigil over a dying world cannot seek exculpation from the hour. He remains a witness. But if Eliot's poetry is foremost that of an anguished heart, the corollary persists — it would make no sense to measure the pained excellence but not locate the object of this emotional turmoil. For no matter the cost, such pain is a shared experience, and the participants are the true witnesses. In either case — that of the artist his age demanded, or the poet of his own obsessions — there emerges a necessary constant, the life of the man. In the face of mounting criticism of Eliot and Pound as poets of degeneration and reactive insularity, whose influence could retreat to a backwater beside the flow of a resilient tradition, it may be prudent to remove from Eliot the mask of the public poet; perhaps take Possum's guise of impersonality with a pinch of salt; and put in their place a wracked, self-preoccupied dandy to see the man plain and understand the greatness of the work in its proper historic context.

In 1956 I'd finished an apprenticeship in bespoke tailoring at Kilgour, French & Stanbury, London; I was fortunate enough to have two early plays *Don't Destroy Me* and *Yes and After* performed in New York. I stayed for some months in the city, and friends provided me with an apartment down on West 14th Street. I was in my eighteenth year, and, for the time, struck an unusual note amidst those towers of capital. I wore suits I had made myself, the odd fingertip-drape jacket with aggressive shoulder-pads and stovepipe trousers, plus a pair of blister-inducing winklepickers with half-moon studs, which made sparks in the dark. It was a glittery time for me. I was compulsively drawn to Harlem, and after my show closed at night I frequently set off uptown to the Black Star province. As it happened, the editor of *The Times Literary Supplement* of the day, Alan Pryce-Jones, had given me an introduction to Edith Sitwell. Eventually I met up with her at an evening for Carson McCullers on 56th Street in early 1957. Conversation steered around a recent wedding in London. The poet T. S. Eliot had, by all accounts, suddenly run off and married his secretary. Not only that, but in the process he had done something quite beastly to John Hayward, a paraplegic with whom he shared rooms. All of this was rather new to the ted who stood there in his winklepicker toes and duck's-arse hairstyle. The old lady held court in an inimical tone, and it appeared that Tom had really let *Edith* down, and she was very upset. There was a reckless and uncaring element within Tom, according to her. What's more, in the distant past he had done something even more beyond the pale. He'd been married to another woman, Vivienne. And, 'At some point in their marriage Tom went mad, and promptly certified his wife.' I toyed with mute fingertip-drape imprimaturs: 'Oh yes, ma'am, sounds like a right-well knackered outragement this does', then thought better of it. Could this be the great poet the Sitwell was criticizing? More like the real rabbit for which Eliot would surely have reserved his best verbals: 'the dourest excruciation'. It was the first I heard about Tom and Viv.

Michael Hastings
Brixton, 1984

TOM AND VIV

Tom and Viv was first performed at the Royal Court Theatre, London, on 3 February 1984. Cast in order of appearance:

Viv	JULIE COVINGTON
Tom/Todd	TOM WILKINSON
Maurice	DAVID HAIG
Louise	DEBORAH FINDLAY
Rose	MARGARET TYZACK
Charles/Janes	NICHOLAS SELBY

Directed by Max Stafford-Clark
Designed by Antony McDonald and Jock Scott
Lighting by Robin Myerscough-Walker
Assistant Director Simon Curtis

CHARACTERS

TOM   aged 26–58
VIVIENNE   26–58
MAURICE   19–51
ROSE   54–73
CHARLES   70–82
LOUISE   21–40

TOM also plays CHARLES MARION TODD, aged 30

CHARLES HAIGH-WOOD also plays WILLIAM LEONARD JANES, aged 80

VOICES: The photographer, the barrister

There are attempted parallels in the doubling; the youthful C. M. Todd is not too far removed from the young Eliot at the start of the play, and Charles Haigh-Wood, as a man who never interfered in his daughter's life, has a reversal of character in the part of W. L. Janes, who was employed to interfere in Viv's life for many years.

CHARACTERS

VIVIENNE ELIOT (1888–1947) Watercolourist (Three Arts Club), modern dancer (Madame Vandyck's Studio), pianist (Royal College of Musicians, and Selfridges self-taught pianoforte), poet and short story writer (the *Criterion*).

TOM ELIOT (1888–1965) Born St Louis, Missouri. Father: President of the Hydraulic Brick Company. Philosophy graduate, Harvard. Sheldon Travelling Scholarship to Oxford, 1915. Poet, publisher and essayist.

MAURICE HAIGH-WOOD (1895–1980) Malvern College and Sandhurst. Assistant Adjutant, 3rd Battalion, Manchester Regiment. Junior partner stockbrokers. Married an American, Ahmé Hoagland, of the Hoagland sisters' cabaret. Invested in iron ore and farmland in East Africa. Moved to West Africa, became Chief of Police, Lagos. Promoted to Lt-Colonel, British Army. Lost half his fortune during the sixties property boom.

ROSE ESTHER ROBINSON HAIGH-WOOD (1861–1941) Born Lincolnshire, one of four sisters. Family had interests in cotton and shipping.

CHARLES HAIGH-WOOD (1845–1927) Landscape artist and portrait painter. Studied at Manchester School of Arts and awarded National Medal in Manchester. Became a member of the Cambrian Academy, and the Royal Watercolour Society. Owner of estates in Dublin.

LOUISE PURDON (1894–1968) M.P.S. (Member of the Pharmaceutical Society) 1915. Became night nurse at Allen & Hanbury's chemist 1921. Joined the National Society for Lunacy Law Reform (North Harrow). Acquired her own chemist shop after 1950. Retired to Deal. Unmarried.

WILLIAM LEONARD JANES (1855–1939) Ex-policeman, security officer for District Bank, Holborn.

CHARLES MARION TODD (1917–50) Rutherford High School, New Jersey. Diploma in Psychological Medicine University of Pennsylvania. Flight surgeon, U.S.A.F. Saxhope, Norfolk. Rockefeller Research Fellow in neurology, Tavistock Clinic, 1946. Stayed with the Army Medical Service to 1950. Attached to the Second Airborne Infantry Division, S.E.A.T.O.; killed on the Pusan Perimeter, South Korea, September 1950.

ACT ONE

Thé dansant, Oxford.

[TOM *and* VIV *have balloons. Music.*]

VIVIENNE: Why aren't you inside chattering to all the dons' wives?

TOM: I don't chatter very well.

VIVJENNE: Or dancing?

TOM: I won't dance.

VIVIENNE: One of these balloons has got a Chinese proverb in it. Whoever's got it wins a bottle of gin.

TOM: I find it an enormous effort to be trivial.

VIVIENNE: Oh dear.

TOM: You aren't mad at me?

VIVIENNE: I was thinking you've possibly reduced your chances of being a social success here at Oxford by a hideous margin. That's all.

TOM: I'm sorry.

VIVIENNE: Why did you come?

TOM: I thought I might catch a glimpse of you.

VIVIENNE: Such a queer boy.

TOM: You do dance in a provocative way. I know all the others just love it.

VIVIENNE: I don't do it for them.

TOM: No.

VIVIENNE: I always know you're there. Watching.

TOM: It's getting cold.

VIVIENNE: Haven't noticed.

TOM: You do get tired so quickly after –

VIVIENNE: Really I'm not.

TOM: I don't want you to be exhausted.

VIVIENNE: Thank you, darling.

TOM: When are we alone?

        [Pause.]

VIVIENNE   *[cockney]*: Cor blimey. Ain't yew a bore. An' no mistake. Cor blimey.

TOM: Oh.

VIVIENNE: And I love you to get out and about. I don't want others to think you're a stick. All right, we could go up to London. The house is empty. Only the staff. And the house is stuffed with cigarettes. So we can be as decadent as we like. The season's coming up. There's Ascot and Goodwood. The Russians at Covent Garden. Daddy never uses the box. We won't have to spend a bean.

TOM: I don't have clothes for all these things.

VIVIENNE: Clothes!

TOM: I don't know these places.

VIVIENNE: What a wonderful time I'll have showing you.

TOM: Please, Vivie!

VIVIENNE: All right.

TOM   *[blurts out]*: I'm deeply touched. I bask in your light. But I can't do all these things. I love you more than life itself. I love you — I . . .

VIVIENNE: Oh dear.

TOM: Excuse me?

VIVIENNE: You don't have to be so wet about it.

TOM: I don't?

VIVIENNE: I'm not on fire or something.

TOM: Oh.

VIVIENNE: I know all that anyway.

        [She takes his arm. Pulls him towards the laughter and music.]

VIVIENNE: Really. Come on. Let's go in. It's a polka. Lots of us. Ever so simple. And jump all about. Make an absolute arse of yourself. No one will care. I won't let go. Tom? Oh, Tom! Plunge! Just plunge!

---

3 Compayne Gardens, Hampstead.

[MAURICE, *19, in uniform. A subaltern, 3rd Manchester Regiment. He is waiting with the drinks.*]

MAURICE: Oh God, Viv. Welcome home.

VIVIENNE: Thank you.

MAURICE: And — congratulations on the marriage. God, it's all been so sudden, hasn't it? Family's in a state of shock really.

VIVIENNE: Mum and Dad?

MAURICE: On the train from Anglesey. Got the telegram this morning. Bringing with them thunder and wrath, I should think. Let's get plastered before they arrive. What do you think of the uniform?

VIVIENNE: I suppose it lends you a shred of distinction.

MAURICE: Oh squelch. That's the old Vivie all right!

VIVIENNE: Is it? I'm not staying.

MAURICE: But you've got to. You can't just elope and not come home and tell us about it.

VIVIENNE: I'm dropping some clothes off I want washed. That's all.

MAURICE: Then there was going to be a filthy family row when Mum and Dad got in. I was looking forward to that.

VIVIENNE: You are a worm.

MAURICE: Anyway — it was a fantastic honeymoon, wasn't it? Bags of candlelight?

VIVIENNE: Bags. I set light to the hotel curtains with them.

MAURICE: And you must have gone out and seen all the sights and stuff.

VIVIENNE: I lay in bed all day with the blinds closed. And I bolted the door.

MAURICE: Oh rather — got stuck into the dreaded sex business.

VIVIENNE: Every night Tom took a rug and slept in a deckchair under the pier. With a bottle of gin.

MAURICE: Ah! I'm dying to meet the Yank. Every family needs a wild crazed sort of black sheep. Does he go in for polka dot ties? And sort of crashing coloured shirts?

[TOM *wears a dark suit. He brings a laundry basket.* TOM *speaks with a New England voice. Tries to be exuberant.*]

... Hallo, sir!

TOM: How do you do?

MAURICE: Absolutely.

TOM: I'm Tom

MAURICE   [*mouth agape*]: ... You are.

TOM: Yes. Well, I was this morning when I woke up.

MAURICE: Of course you are! God, I'm rude. You must excuse me. I'm
           Maurice.

TOM: The *fratris*?

MAURICE: Sir?

TOM: Brother-in-law.

MAURICE: Ah. Yes. *Fratris*. My Greek's not up to much these days.

TOM: Latin.

MAURICE: Ah.

VIVIENNE: Squelch.

MAURICE: I ... I've just been hearing about the honeymoon. It's been
           ripping, hasn't it?

TOM: Yes. We're enormously happy. I'm a very proud man.
                [TOM *puts an arm around* VIVIENNE.]

MAURICE: It's all been such massive fun.

TOM   [*tuning into* MAURICE]: Massive.

MAURICE: I ... I gather you're going to be the poet in the family. I'm afraid
           I'm pretty much a conservative in that area. I wondered if your
           poems rhyme?

TOM: Massively.

MAURICE: Course, all things don't have to rhyme —

TOM: I've written a racy little ballad about King Bolo and his big black
           hairy kween/whose bum is as big as a soup tureen. Will that
           do?

MAURICE: Rather.

TOM   [*exuberant*]: How about King Bolo's big black bastard kween/
           That airy fairy hairy 'un./She led the dance on Golders Green/
           With half a jew boy's knickers on — ?

MAURICE: Oh grand.

TOM: King Bolo's big black hairy kween/Had a brightly coloured
           sphincter/She wiped her bum with tangerine/And swallowed
           saffron tincture.

MAURICE: Oh pretty hot stuff, poetry!

M + L

TOM: Why thank you, Maurice.

MAURICE: I'm rather keen on Robert Service. 'The Ballad of Blasphemous
          Bill'? Know that by heart. Shall I give a rendition − ?

VIVIENNE [*moving*]: Goodbye, Maurice.

MAURICE: No wait. I don't mean to be a squelch. Honest.

VIVIENNE: Tell Mummy I've left the laundry basket.

MAURICE: I'm awfully sorry, Tom. My mind's jammed with useless bits of
          info. Isn't yours?
               [*Holds up the bottle.*]
               . . . You can't leave like this! What am I going to say to Mum
          and Dad? A toast! What?
               [*He pops the cork.*]
               . . . To Tom and Viv on their ripping honeymoon!
               [VIV *doesn't drink.*]

TOM: . . . At night, Eastbourne pier possesses one hundred and fourteen
          uprights which stand clear of the sea. The tide comes in at
          dawn, thus reducing this number to twenty-eight.
               [*Lights.*]

Allen & Hanbury's chemist, Finchley Road.

               [LOUISE PURDON, *19, has two bottles and a prescription form.
               She wears crisp cotton with a starched nursing cap.* VIVIENNE
               enters.]

LOUISE: Mrs Eliot?

VIVIENNE: Yes.

LOUISE: Prescription. The anodyne and the bromide.

VIVIENNE: Thank you.

LOUISE: Excuse me for asking − I noticed it was signed by Sir Frederick
          Treves − that's the King's personal physician, innit?

VIVIENNE: He's also mine.

LOUISE: Hope you won't mind me saying so − this is what Sir Fred
          recommends, isn't it? Course it is. I know. But − this anodyne
          is sixty per cent spirit of ether. And the bromide is ninety per
          cent alcohol.

VIVIENNE: Well, what about it?

LOUISE: Hope you won't think I'm too keen but – when taken together these compounds have a dangerous effect.

VIVIENNE: You think the King's personal physician erred in some way?

LOUISE: Oh please, no! See I'm new here. I just wanted you to know like. That you take these doses with care. Course you know that. Me an' my big mouth, ma'am.

VIVIENNE: Thank you.

LOUISE: My first week this is. That's why I talk so. Terrified. I want to become night nurse. The senior chemist here says girls ain't reliable enough for such posts. That ain't true, ma'am, is it?

VIVIENNE: May I go now?

LOUISE: That'll be one shilling and fourpence, ma'am.

    [*She gives the bottles to* VIVIENNE.]

VIVIENNE: The account is in my mother's name. Mrs Haigh-Wood.

    [*They leave.*]

    [ROSE HAIGH-WOOD *steps forward.*]

ROSE: We have a manor house on Anglesey which we keep for the summer. We close up the London home and take all dogs, maids and children. My husband has estates in Dublin. He is also a landscape artist. He finds a lot to paint on Anglesey. But this year was different. Vivie had gone to Oxford with an American friend, Tom. She was not at Oxford, of course. She was staying with some friends. Out of the blue came a telegram. Tom and Viv had run off and married in a registry place. Vivie had contrived it to spite me. With her medical history she knew I would have to put a stop to it. And I was especially afraid for young Tom.

---

3 Compayne Gardens, Hampstead.

    [ROSE *is seated.* TOM *walks in. Bowler and umbrella.*]

TOM: I won't excuse what we've done. I can't apologize for being in love with Vivie. She's married me on nothing. I owe her everything. I am convinced she is the right person. She has made this sacrifice. She is my life. I ... don't know what else to do.

'Me, Mummy, Dad and Vivie in London, 1906. You can detect the rather dandyish Bohemian side to Dad. He didn't have to wear that high stiff collar. Vivie is seventeen here. Mummy liked to get about. Skiing in Austria at Christmas, Anglesey in fine weather. Dad kept another house and studio to paint in down in Buckinghamshire. What with the house in London, couple of dozen villas at Kingspoint, outside Dublin – Dad had all these buildings, none of them what you might call absolutely kept up. Oh, chandeliers and Georgian furniture…'

– Maurice Haigh-Wood

Vivienne Haigh-Wood, Plas Llanfair, Anglesey, 1914.
'The family kept up this absurd place. Very damp. Thick walls... Cold dank evenings. God, I used to admire Viv then. She'd play the piano and sing. And invent wonderful family games. Write stunning sort of instant doggerel rhymes. And dress up. And then dance in the candlelight for Dad. And he'd make drawings of her. Her laugh – bit high-pitched. She'd suddenly be tired. And we'd all be left flat.'

– Maurice Haigh-Wood

'I was seventeen. Final term at Malvern, 1912. Vivie descended on the school. Oh, rigged up to the minute. Crêpe de Chine tie, white collar, striped shirt like a man. She gushed like hell about London, the Hippodrome, the music hall turns, plans to see Karsavina and Nijinsky when they arrived. The other boys dropped their jaws and gaped. She insisted on taking us all out for a tremendous tea in town. And she goes and does a cartwheel on the lawn right in front of the housemaster's res. I just died. She was twenty-four.'

– Maurice Haigh-Wood

'William Leonard Janes, 1930. Gave the impression of the military type – backbone of the nation. Tom loved that...Mummy claimed Janes always reminded her of a lavatory attendant down the public gents.'

– Maurice Haigh-Wood

Louise Purdon, 1935

'Yes. Tom and me discussing the horses, 1929. What I liked about him the way he stood up to it when a bet went wrong. Confused, rather quizzical look on his face, not quite believing this nag had dunned him in the four-thirty. It wasn't always just the horses. He was determined to get close up to the Duke of Kent. So he and Vivie and this poet Hodgson actually ran right across the course one day. And the race still in progress. I thought, steady on.'

– Maurice Haigh-Wood

'Here we are in Italy, 1926. [*Left to right: Viv, Ahmé, Maurice, Tom*] Tom and Viv had their best rows in restaurants. Tremendous stuff. Sort of howling tea cups. Whenever they got going – God, total blistering. Viv on Mussolini and Umberto. She was saying Mussolini was a fascist because his roots were common. Tom was saying Mussolini was an interesting fascist precisely because he'd thrown up socialism. There was development, sort of thing. Vivie wouldn't have any of this. She had this theory about the working class being natural fascists. Tom said fascism is a form of growth and change. Viv was spitting. And Tom's satin hank in his breastpocket had gone limp with the heat. They were still hammer and tong back at the hotel. Until Tom and Viv got to their bedroom. Then it was dead silence. I don't think Mussolini had anything to do with it.'

– Maurice Haigh-Wood

Vivienne Haigh-Wood Eliot, 1933. She wears a *Phillipe et Gaston* outfit on her way to meet the Prince of Wales. It was at the peak of the crisis in the Eliot marriage and during their separation.

ROSE: You could of course – sit down.

TOM: I'm so sorry, Mrs Haigh-Wood –

ROSE: And do something sensible with that hat and brolly –

TOM: I didn't mean to hurt you –

ROSE: Lemon?

TOM: Thank you.
       [*Takes a cup.*]

ROSE: You know, Hampstead at this time of the year is crammed with people making confessions to one another. That's why I like to get away. Anglesey is very different.

TOM: Really.

ROSE: I so hoped we could have an ordinary chat about the little things. How was the wedding?

TOM: Just a very civil affair.

ROSE: Any witnesses?

TOM: Lucy Thayer and Pam Butler.

ROSE: Vivie wear white?

TOM: No.

ROSE: Very sensible. Then you went to Eastbourne?

TOM: We booked the Lansdowne for two weeks. After six nights the money ran out.

ROSE: Oh dear. It's lovely to find a good hotel. And nice discreet staff. But these places are frightfully expensive. Was it a sunny room?

TOM: We hardly had a moment indoors to find out.

ROSE: Ah –

TOM: We spent hours up on the Wish Tower roof watching the boats. It's a ten-minute brisk walk to the pier each day. Very bracing for Vivie. And the band on Grand Parade played for free. Nigger minstrels on the prom in the evening. Like Forest Park in St Louis on Thanksgiving.

ROSE: The pride of Eastbourne is you won't find one shop window on the front.

TOM: Behind the hotel there's a track across the downs. It's a walk to Jevington village. The track stops at the edge of a field. There's a public house there, just across the stile. On the way back. Cowslip and fruit in the hedgerows. Had to wash the blackberries in our room. So much salt in the air.

ROSE: Bliss.

TOM: That's right.

> [ROSE *opens a typed letter*.]

ROSE   [*reading*]:

> Dear Madame
>
> Thank you for the return of the sheets and hand towels which belong to room 86. During her short stay, Mrs Eliot insisted on changing all linen herself. The chambermaid tried to gain access. But the doors were somehow barracked. There are marks on a chest of drawers. A curtain is burned. A window pane is missing. Under these circumstances, Mr Eliot behaved with such forbearance, the management has decided not to press for reparation.
>
> Yours faithfully
>
> Messrs Lansdowne Hotel
>
> Eastbourne
>
> ... Before she rushed you into this. Headlong. What did she tell you?

TOM: Nothing.

ROSE   [*stands*]: I am enormously proud of you. I think you are going to make a wonderful member of the family. And you and me will keep our little secret.

> [CHARLES HAIGH-WOOD *and* MAURICE *enter*.]

CHARLES: Hallo, Tom. Let's get this nonsense over and done with. You're both twenty-six. None of my business what you do. Is she pregnant?

TOM: No, sir.

CHARLES: After her money?

TOM: I wasn't aware she had any.

CHARLES: Are you a Johnny-come-lately?

TOM: Excuse me – ?

MAURICE: Cad – bounder –

TOM: Not to my knowledge, no –

CHARLES: What does Mr Eliot say?

TOM: He's withheld my allowance.

CHARLES: Get anything from Harvard?

TOM: Hundred dollars a year.

CHARLES: Oh?

TOM: To finish a paper on Bradley. F. H. Bradley is a philosopher. He believes the whole is greater than the sum of its parts.

ROSE: The very last thing my husband will want to hear about is someone else's philosophy.

CHARLES: Got a roof?

TOM: A small room in Bloomsbury.

CHARLES: Got a Club?

TOM: Harvard Dramatic.

CHARLES: What is your ambition?

TOM: I have no idea.

CHARLES: Got a religion?

TOM: I've ceased being a Unitarian. A Unitarian –

ROSE: You'll find it an uphill task trying to explain any religion to him. He finds them all equally confusing.

CHARLES: Now – eh –

ROSE: Try prospects.

CHARLES: Well?

TOM: None whatsoever.

            [CHARLES *is silent.*]

ROSE: Followed by intentions.

CHARLES: Yes?

TOM: I believe family unity is the root of all culture. Vivie is my life. I'll care for her always.

CHARLES: Ah . . .

ROSE   [*to* TOM]: Much too serious. Let's keep life on a social level.

CHARLES: Any special talent?

ROSE: And we don't brag.

TOM   [*glances at* MAURICE]: I – have a feeling for ditties which rhyme.

ROSE: That's better.

CHARLES: Well then. Now I've got a very good bottle of sherry tucked away somewhere – to celebrate –

ROSE   [*to* TOM]: He means he's extremely relieved you haven't stung him for a champagne supper at the Savoy for five hundred Eliots and Haigh-Woods. And in his curious way he's trying to tell you he approves.

CHARLES: You see my wife loves to treat me as if I'm the imbecile of the family. I suppose I do take things with a pinch of salt. Life on a duck's back. Do you like Landseer?

ROSE: Nice and light.

TOM: I've – glimpsed his lions in Trafalgar Square.

CHARLES: Ever read G. Whyte Melville?

TOM: I have dipped into them.

MAURICE: I've read the lot.

CHARLES: Best horse and hound writer in the business.

ROSE [*to* TOM]: Just say you think the horses have well-rounded three-dimensional characters and we can get out of this one in no time. How small did you say this room is you've got?

TOM: Well, it is small.

MAURICE: Jolly romantic, small.

TOM: We met an old tutor of mine. Bertie Russell has a flat in Bury Street. He insisted we share it with him. It's a room behind the kitchen where he stores china. It's large enough for a single cot, and there's a davenport. Sometimes I sleep in a deckchair in the hall.

ROSE: I once danced with a Bertie Russell, in Ostend.

TOM: I don't want any of you to be shocked. But Bertie is the Honourable Bertrand Russell. He's chairman of the No-Conscription Fellowship.

CHARLES: Oh – the Bolshevik. The seducer. Bertie who the *Express* calls 'the most hated man in London'. Why should I be shocked? He's most probably a member of the Junior Carlton and I bump into him once a week.

ROSE: Doesn't sound like the Bertie I danced with.

TOM: If I could lay your mind at rest. I've applied for a teaching job. And I have an offer of six lectures on 'French Symbolism'.

CHARLES: Two dollars a week. There's this crockery cupboard you share with the most hated man in London. There are six French symbols somewhere. And a deckchair. And not a prospect in sight. Nothing could make me feel more secure. Can I go back to Anglesey now?

> [VIVIENNE *has two hatboxes. She wears a smock of Bohemia,* rive gauche *beret and cravat.*]

VIVIENNE: ... Mum, Dad!

           [*Hands out leaflets. Drops the boxes.*]

           ... the ... No-Conscription Fellowship wants your support. Britain will honour its pact with Belgium and France. But no more. Tens of thousands are dead. Half a million tons of shipping sunk. Three million troops are enough! Stop it now!

           [MAURICE *is in uniform. She offers him a leaflet.*]

CHARLES: [*to* VIV]: So how is the Honourable Bertie?

VIVIENNE: Bertie just dropped me off. Intense crush at Selfridges. Couldn't get him away from the hat department. Wrenching spit with the salesgirl. I told her she was serving the world's foremost mathematician. She said she couldn't help that. The gentleman she said had counted wrong. There was one and tuppence missing. Anyway. Fell into a taxi cab. The cabbie looks round. 'Ere! Excuse I, guv. But ain't you the 'Onoroable Bertrand Russell, the world's greatest 'uman thinker of general knowledge? Well, guv, my question is – wot's it all abaht?'

           [*Swift change in mood.*] War is utterly brutal. And you are going to send Maurice, and he is going to die!

CHARLES: Ask her to stop.

TOM: Vivienne!

VIVIENNE: The good news is that Bertie has paid for my dance classes for a year. The War Office in its wisdom has banned Bertie from Bristol, Clydeside and the village of Sandringham. But he has promised to take me to the last corner of England he's allowed in. He wants to give away three thousand pounds' worth of shares in a munition factory. Investment in war is a crime. Absentee landlords are vermin to be put down.

MAURICE: That is filthy nonsense.

CHARLES: Thank you, Vivie.

VIVIENNE: These are my men – Tom and Bertie. But they cannot communicate. I unlock their minds. Poor Tom, life lingers for him. So I make him race on past it with me, together ...

           [*Swift change again.*] Everybody in this room is dead. You are parchment and dust. I will never come back.

ROSE: Please ... ? I think Vivie would like to talk to me.

           [*She ushers out* MAURICE *and* TOM *and* CHARLES.]

ROSE: ... Very still.
                 [VIVIENNE *is silent.*]
                 ... Very calm.
                 [VIVIENNE *is silent.*]
                 ... And you could hear what you were saying?
VIVIENNE: Yes.
                 [VIVIENNE *regains. Pause.*]
ROSE: Was Tom a virgin?
VIVIENNE: Yes.
ROSE: He's not quite what I imagined a poet to be.
VIVIENNE: Sorry, Mummy.
ROSE: And he's not quite one of us.
VIVIENNE: Sorry.
ROSE: I only want you to lead a decent life.
VIVIENNE: Mummy, try all you like. You can't stop it now. Tom is mine.
                 Whatever.
ROSE: ... Let's talk about the other business.
VIVIENNE: Bertie said —
ROSE: And nothing more! You understand?
                 [VIVIENNE *gathers herself.*]
VIVIENNE: ... I take the pills for my head. The tummy comes back. I take
                 the liquid for the tummy. The head is back. Sometimes I take
                 them all at once. I know I'm not supposed to, but I ...
ROSE: How often does Granny visit you?
VIVIENNE: I thought Granny was dead.
ROSE: Very well — how often do you get the curse?
VIVIENNE: Twice — three times.
ROSE: In a month?
VIVIENNE: Yes, but it isn't like Granny, it's a little pinkness. I call it my pinky
                 pale little flowers. The more often things get frightful, the
                 more often there is a flower or two.
ROSE: You ... have a lot of off-days?
VIVIENNE: Yes.
ROSE: You have a plentiful supply of S.T.s?
VIVIENNE: Yes, I have so many sanitary towels I could make a Canadian
                 patchwork eiderdown.
ROSE: That is not nice.

VIVIENNE: In two colours!

ROSE: Vivienne!

> [VIVIENNE *is silent.*]

> I try so hard not to use nasty words. It is something others don't like to hear. At school, I always covered for you. Whenever it was called for − I sent a note to your headmistress. You remember? 'Vivie's grandma is here.' And it was understood.

VIVIENNE: Grannie has overstayed her welcome.

ROSE: These are nasty things, darling.

> [VIVIENNE *is silent.*]

> They are not easy to put into words.

> [VIVIENNE *is silent.*]

> And most off-putting for a husband.

VIVIENNE: Yes.

ROSE: One can only go so far.

> [VIVIENNE *tidies herself.*]

> Of course, I don't want to find fault. But I'm certain this doesn't come from my side of the family.

VIVIENNE: I should think Dad'll be glad to hear that.

> [*Lights.* ROSE *steps forward.*]

ROSE: The Honourable Bertie bought her dresses and pressed her with jewels which were family heirlooms. She was swept off her feet. He took her to the Torbay Hotel for a holiday. What were we to believe? She wanted the affair. When she got back to London I sent Maurice round with the car, with instructions to fetch Tom and Vivie immediately.

> [*Lights.*]

---

34 Russell Chambers, Bury Street.

> [TOM *is cross-legged by the door. Beside boxes and cases.* MAURICE *edges forward with all his military skill. He holds a lighter flame.*]

MAURICE: ... Light bulb gone ... top floor ... Bolshevik and most hated man in London.

TOM: Pull yourself together, Maurice.

MAURICE: How is she?

TOM: A little better.

MAURICE: And the indescribable letch?

TOM: He's gone to the Lake District.

MAURICE: I hear he likes to swim out to a raft with a girl, then he strips right down. Ghastly. So he's squelched off?

TOM: I saw him off.

MAURICE: Hope you smote him to his palsied knees.

TOM: Not quite.

MAURICE: Course. I bet you were more subtle. Gave him such a tongue-lashing strips peeled off.

TOM: I said goodbye.

MAURICE: Ah.

TOM: He said goodbye.

MAURICE: Sort of ice-cold daggers.

TOM: He kissed her. And I hugged him.

MAURICE: Lor'.

TOM: Bertie loves us very much as if we were his children. He is an astonishing friend. I think the world of him.

> [VIVIENNE *opens the door. Tosses out a packed suitcase. Slams door.*]

MAURICE: ... Staff's made something splendid for tea. Can't wait to have you home.

TOM: Thank you.

MAURICE: Specially Viv. Bit like end of term.

TOM: You must have been very close.

MAURICE: Oh peas in the pod.

TOM: My older sister once told me every secret she possessed.

MAURICE: Perhaps not that close. We both boarded out. Well – we hardly ever met.

TOM: I see.

MAURICE: I mean – there was seven years between us. I was never told. You have to understand I'm the earwig of the family.

TOM: That's all right, Maurice.

MAURICE: Fact is – I was at Sandhurst last year. Vivie got engaged. Then Mum told his family Vivie couldn't lead a normal life. When I got home it was all over. I never even met the chap.

TOM: But you knew?

MAURICE: Oh in the end. Ear to the ground really. You see in our family
           you learn to say *nothing at all.* Not a murmur in a house of
           mutes sort of thing. And all will be revealed.

           [VIVIENNE *opens the door. Pushes out hatboxes and valises.
           Slams door.*]

           ... What with all Vivie's medical bills, I had to settle for
           Malvern College. Sort of one point below Dulwich and two
           points up on Bedford. You can't get much lower than Bedford.
           Where were you?

TOM: St Louis, Missouri. Bedford wins.

MAURICE: I wanted to ask you what sort of form you had. But with a Yank
           you can't really do that. I mean we've been Irish landlords
           since Cromwell.

TOM: There's an Eliot who burned half the witches of Salem. And an
           Eliot who founded Harvard University. Is that form enough
           for Cromwell?

           [VIVIENNE *opens the door. Slings out smaller items. Coats etc.*]

MAURICE: What do you think of our English cockneys?

TOM: Dickens to a fault.

MAURICE: And our London fog?

TOM: Very Conan Doyle.

           [TOM's *irritation.*]

MAURICE: I do like you and things, Tom. I want you and Vivie to fight
           through and win. Staff's made up the best bedroom at home.
           Separate beds of course. Can't wait.

TOM: You won't mind if I tell you I've never met someone quite as
           stupid?

MAURICE: Eh –

TOM: At first I didn't grasp you. Now I've really begun to admire you –

MAURICE: I say –

TOM: You've turned ignorance on a massive scale into a virtue.

MAURICE: Oh pax, Tom.

TOM: I go through life seeking intelligence and purpose. What you've
           got is a ready-made system which requires the minimum of
           maintenance. No spare parts needed. Oh, there is the occa-
           sional English inventiveness. But on the whole you're the

machine Mr Henry Ford has looked for all his life. You're an embodiment, Maurice. You do understand?

MAURICE   [hurt]: Eh – not a word, actually.

TOM: It's this closed order you possess. As if by right. A kind of remission of the mind. You say you will – you won't. Say you can't – you can. Say what you really mean – you don't at all. And when there's a chance to say nothing – you grab at silence with the speed of light. You've no idea how much I envy you. I haven't quite learned the trick. I should have gone to Malvern. Or was it Bedford?

MAURICE: I ... join the regiment on Monday. Boat's leaving for Aden. Gallipoli next. Three out of four junior officers don't come back they say.

TOM: Let's not settle down into self-reflection. Doesn't suit you at all.

MAURICE: No ... none of my business really, but ... man to man, Tom?

TOM: All right?

MAURICE: Is there something beastly and quite bloody awful between you and Viv?

TOM: *Nothing. Nothing at all.*

MAURICE: Well done, sir.

TOM: Is that the trick, Maurice?

MAURICE: Rather.

            [VIVIENNE *stands in the doorway. She holds two letters and a certificate of shares.*

            MAURICE *and* TOM *pick up the cases.*]

VIVIENNE   [*to* MAURICE]: ... Ask him to take this down to the car.

            [*She pushes the vanity-case towards* MAURICE.

            TOM *and* MAURICE *clear.*

            VIVIENNE *holds up the letters. The laundry basket remains.*]

VIVIENNE: Dear Tom

            You knew you'd have to forgive me if we went to Torquay. That was our arrangement. I am now in the unenviable position of having not gone far enough. Seduction did not take place. Frankly, I was afraid. Vivie lives on a knife edge. There is something in her which will turn her into a saint or a criminal. If you won't share your life with her, she will strike back in a most extraordinary way. Please find enclosed the

munition bonds which will provide you with an income for
the duration of the war.

Ever yours

Bertie

P.S. Hide your reply in the usual place.

P.P.S. There isn't a sheet left in the place. Will you pop round
to the Chinese Laundry in Coptic Street?

VIVIENNE: Dear Bertie

I thank you with all my heart. If you hadn't taken her away
I'd have broken in pieces. She needs and deserves a love that
I cannot give her. But I am at an end. I dare not imagine what
future we possess.

[TOM *enters again.*]:

Your munition bonds.

[*Lights.*]

MAURICE   [*introduces*]: PART TWO 1921

18 *Crawford Mansions.*

[VIVIENNE *takes out a Hoover and lead. Plugs it in. Knock on the door.*]
LOUISE: Hallo, Ma'am.
VIVIENNE: Come in, Louie.
LOUISE: I thought I'd bring the medicines over.
VIVIENNE: Thank you.
LOUISE: Each bottle has separate instructions. I thought perhaps you'd like me to go over them with you?
VIVIENNE: I can read. I'm not that ill you know!
            [VIVIENNE *switches on the Hoover. There is a bang. Both jump.*]
            These new appliances just won't go. Tom will never believe this happened by accident. I washed the toaster last week. That blew up. Can you mend a Hoover by any chance, Louie?
LOUISE   [*touches*]: There's olive oil dripping out of it.
VIVIENNE: Oh yes, well. I put that on it to speed it up.
            [*Both laugh. Lights.*]

The Warrior House Hotel, St Leonards.

[CHARLES *in a wheelchair.*]
CHARLES: Wife acquires taste for Japanese wallpaper. Son rejected by stockbrokers on account of brain capacity. Son-in-law turns pauper, and takes six years to produce two slim volumes of verse. Daughter takes to frenzied movements at dance studio. After the war, there was a need to be silly again. A sense of respite. Tom joined my Club. And ran up a bill at the tailors. My tailors. I quickly found him a job at a bank. Sometimes Tom and Viv played bridge with us at home. Unusual system of play. They'd sit opposite in silence, and kick each other's shins beneath the table. Been struck low by a filthy illness. Retreated to the Warrior House Hotel, St Leonards. The

children come down and take turns to read verses to me. I hate
verse. I hate being read to.

[VIVIENNE *and* TOM *enter.* CHARLES *looks up.*]

TOM: Vivie and I will read extracts from work-in-progress.

CHARLES [*softly*]: I ... can't think of anything I'd like better.

VIVIENNE: Tom has chosen a working title:

CHARLES: Oh good.

TOM: It's called 'He Do the Police in Different Voices'.

CHARLES: Well ... if there's one thing you need, it's a catchy title.

TOM: The poem is very long.

CHARLES: I'm sure it is.

VIVIENNE: You must realize Tom quotes from a dozen other poets and
stories. You have to think of poetry as if it is a smashed vase.

CHARLES: Oh – all the time.

VIVIENNE: The central voice in the poem is Tiresias the prophet. He sees
Athena's body naked. It is such a frightful shock he thinks of
nothing but rats in a sewer.

TOM: I don't think the poem needs –

VIVIENNE [*to* CHARLES]: And there are other voices which emerge. The
duchess from the Webster play. She made a reckless marriage
to Antonio. Her family go to any length to stop it. There is
a moment when she brushes her hair. And he cannot touch
her. The horror engulfs him.

TOM: That's not what I meant at all –

VIVIENNE: I mean it is right to explain how the poem works. I want
Daddy to understand what the voices say.

TOM: Please, Vivie –

VIVIENNE [*to* CHARLES]: Tom quotes from Dante. The woman La Pia has
married a soldier. Soon after the wedding he found out he's
made a hideous mistake.

CHARLES: Is ... there anything more I need to know before I hear the
poem?

VIVIENNE: I may burst out with a ritual incantation.

CHARLES: Ah.

VIVIENNE: Weyira wyria wy-a wy-a wy-a ...!
[*It is shrill. Pause.*]

CHARLES: And what is that?

VIVIENNE: The cry of the Rhinemaiden from *Götterdämmerung*.

CHARLES: Well, of course it is, Vivie. How could it possibly be anything
           else?

           [*Pause.*]

VIVIENNE: You do want us to read the poem?

CHARLES: Can't wait.

VIVIENNE: Under the firelight, under the brush, her hair
           Spread out in fiery points
           Glowed into words, then would be savagely still.
           My nerves are bad tonight. Yes, bad. Stay with me.
           Speak to me. Why do you never speak?
           Speak.
           What are you thinking of? What thinking?
           What?
           I never know what you are thinking. Think.

TOM: I think we are in rats' alley
       Where the dead men lost their bones.

The Schiffs' house, Porchester Terrace.

           [MAURICE *and* ROSE *dance off stage. They dance back on. The
           dress sword wrecks their steps. The band stops.*]

ROSE: I'd forgotten what a gifted dancer you were.

MAURICE: Pretty difficult to persuade anyone here to dance. I went up
           to this ravishing thing just now. She said she didn't dance with
           soldiers. Then I found this other creature by the bar. And she
           said she didn't dance with men at all. Life is thin, Mummy.

ROSE: It's too much of Vivie to invite us here. And never turn up.
        I don't even know what the host looks like.

MAURICE: Oh, pretty rich Jews. House is crammed with masterpieces.
           They'll show up.

ROSE: That's beside the point.

MAURICE: Anyway, the booze is ace.

           [VIVIENNE. *Tomboy trews. Polished brogues. Fitted jacket. Flat-
           cap. Tie.*]

VIVIENNE: ... There you are, hiding! Hallo, Mums!

ROSE: You can't imagine what an unpleasant time we've had. Where were you?

VIVIENNE: Tom was late from work. We took an age changing.

ROSE: Yes, but –

VIVIENNE: You must be enjoying yourselves. Isn't it marvellous?

MAURICE: Awfully nice of you to ask us, Vivie.

VIVIENNE: I wanted you to see what we get up to. I mean these are our friends. These are the sort of people we've come to know.

MAURICE: Nice if Tom joins us.

VIVIENNE: Course he will. He knows you're here.

MAURICE: I don't suppose you could fill us in on your get-up?

VIVIENNE: I'm Dr Crippen's mistress.

ROSE: That is a perfectly horrible idea.

VIVIENNE: Tom thinks it's brilliant.

ROSE: Oh dear.

VIVIENNE: Crippen's wife was a nightmare to live with. He couldn't bear to touch her. He poisoned her and cut her into pieces. I am the typist he fell in love with. We ran off to Canada and on the boat I dressed up as a boy.

ROSE: I'm so glad your father isn't here.

VIVIENNE: Perhaps you'd like to guess who's dressed up as Dr Crippen?

ROSE: I don't think I want to know, dear.

VIVIENNE: Tom's in the other room. Go and see?

ROSE: I'd rather not.

VIVIENNE: It's all my idea.

ROSE: I'm sure it is.

VIVIENNE: Come on, Mums – you do like the party?

ROSE: I shouldn't have come here.

VIVIENNE: Mums, I'll take you round the room – I'll –

ROSE: The place is filled with opinionated types doing their utmost to be nasty to each other. In all the time I've been here, I've exchanged four words with the wine waiter and I've had a perfectly bloody tango with my son's regimental cutlass. There isn't a face I can put a name to.

VIVIENNE: Mums, a Marie Antoinette costume doesn't go down too well here.

MAURICE: Tom will join us, won't he?

VIVIENNE: Course he will. Look, Mums — let me show you who they are. You did say you wanted to see new faces. Over there, in the black tights and the lemonade tutu, you remember, the most hated man in London?

ROSE: No wonder I'm not enjoying this party.

VIVIENNE: Those two boys are the most promising writers of the day. Both went to Eton. Both to Oxford. And they're renowned pederasts. In the summer they take youth parties to the Tyrol. And drink hot chocolate in very small tents.

ROSE: Dear, I'm not the least surprised.

VIVIENNE: They have a flat in Charing Cross. Tom keeps a room there. When he wants to get away.

ROSE: You can't shock me, you know.

VIVIENNE: Now that ostrich inside a bedquilt is Ottoline. She thinks I take away Tom's muse. Poor woman. I am his muse.

ROSE: It's all right Vivie —

VIVIENNE: The woman there. With the Kaiser Bill helmet. You've heard of Miss Mansfield from New Zealand. Who writes stories.

ROSE: Darling —

VIVIENNE: She walks out of a room if I come in. She —

ROSE: I don't think I ought to be here.

VIVIENNE   [points]: And that one there in the Mad March Hare suit. That's Mrs Woolf. She meets Tom in secret. She wants him to leave me. She calls me a 'bag of ferrets'.

ROSE: I don't know when to ask you to stop, Vivie.

VIVIENNE: I wanted you to see our friends —

ROSE: I'm afraid for you, darling.

VIVIENNE: Tom is dying to see you.

ROSE: I'll go home now.

[ROSE retreats.]

VIVIENNE: Oh but, Mummy —

ROSE: It's so difficult to believe what you say. Can you understand that?

[ROSE kisses MAURICE. Hurries away.]

... Good-night, Maurice.

VIVIENNE: ... Mummy, please!

ROSE   [stops, turns back]: I am so afraid.

[*Leaves.* VIVIENNE *turns. She sits beside* MAURICE *on the rattan chairs. Music.*
Pause.]

MAURICE: It's an ace party, Viv.

VIVIENNE: Thank you.

MAURICE: Everyone's ace cultured here.

VIVIENNE: That's right.

MAURICE: They know absolutely what they're doing. That's what I admire.

VIVIENNE: Good.

MAURICE: I can see Tom. Got his stethoscope on his chest. Makes a marvellous Dr Crippen. What's he got in the black bag?

VIVIENNE: Stink bombs.

MAURICE: Awfully clever is Tom.

VIVIENNE: Clever.

MAURICE: I mean I know you have your ups and downs. But sort of in between the inbetween parts you must be jolly happy.

VIVIENNE: Happy.

MAURICE: Just for a moment I thought he saw us. He's turned round and gone back into the ballroom.

VIVIENNE: Do something – will you?

MAURICE: Course. Anything.

VIVIENNE: I want you to come home with us. Just tonight. Tom and I ... aren't really very good at being alone together ...

[*Distant music. It fades away. Lights.*]

---

18 Crawford Mansions, Crawford Street.

[*Lights up. The next morning. A sofa with its back to us. A jacket, a waistcoat and a tie on chair. A screen conceals an occasional table. On the table a brolly, gloves, briefcase and bowler.* TOM *in vest and trousers. He studies a shirt before he puts it on.* VIVIENNE *enters. She has a dressing-gown.*]

TOM: Where is the office shirt?

VIVIENNE: It isn't dry.

[TOM's *quiet despair.*]

TOM: This will have to do.

VIVIENNE: The collar's got grime.

TOM: And there's just time for a cup of tea.

VIVIENNE: I had no money for the shopping.

TOM: Well then, I'll grab a cup at the station.

            [*He pulls on his shirt.*]

VIVIENNE: Nobody goes to work after a party like that.

TOM: I envy them.

VIVIENNE: Where is my cheque book?

TOM: I've made one out for £3. You can take it to the bank and sign it.

            [*He takes out a book of cheques. Peels off a top one. Gives it to her.*]

VIVIENNE: So shall we make out a shopping list?

TOM: It's done.

            [*He takes out a list of items and hands it to her.*]

VIVIENNE: You've left out the chocolate.

TOM: I know a special shop.

VIVIENNE: I haven't forgotten about tonight.

TOM: No ...

VIVIENNE: What shall I wear?

TOM: What you see fit.

VIVIENNE: Six o'clock at the Grafton?

TOM: There's a private bar. I'll be with Lady Rothermere. You order a drink and wait in the foyer. When we've finished our business, I'll give you a wave. You can stop by and be introduced.

            [TOM *looks around him.*]

            Time I went.

VIVIENNE: Goodbye.

TOM: Have you seen the umbrella?

VIVIENNE: I'm afraid it's gone.

TOM: And my hat?

VIVIENNE: That's also gone.

TOM: The gloves and the briefcase – I imagine they've gone too?

VIVIENNE: Yes.

TOM: You know I can't go to work without them Vivie.

VIVIENNE: I do.

TOM: Therefore I really need them. There are overseas bonds which
        do not belong to me. I'm sure you don't want me to say I've
        mislaid these things.

VIVIENNE: I have this dreadful confession.

TOM: Confess.

VIVIENNE: I ... was so ill last night when I got back. I was doing things
        in the kitchen. I don't know what happened to me. I threw
        a number of things down the rubbish shute. An umbrella, yes,
        I know there was an umbrella. And I can't get them back until
        the porter turns up.

        [TOM *moves towards her. She stands closer to the screen. He
        hesitates. Walks behind the screen. He picks up the gloves and
        the umbrella and bowler.* TOM *moves towards her.* VIVIENNE
        moves aside from him.]

TOM: Shall we say at the Grafton at six?

VIVIENNE: What a good idea.

        [MAURICE *emerges from the back of the sofa. He has his
        regimental dress on. But crumpled.*]

TOM: ... Good morning, Maurice.

MAURICE: ... My head!

TOM: Sleep well?

MAURICE: Not a lot.

TOM: I hope we didn't keep you awake?

MAURICE: Gosh no –

TOM: I thought perhaps –

MAURICE: I can listen to people all night. Goes in one and flies out the
        other sort of thing.

TOM: Goes in one ear?

MAURICE: That's it.

TOM: And out the other?

MAURICE: Like a shot.

TOM: Yes.

MAURICE: Just like life. really.

TOM: Yes.

MAURICE   [*a little uncertain*]: Rather.

TOM   [*grinding*]: You insufferable oaf! ... Help us!

        [VIVIENNE *turns away. Lights.*]

The Warrior House Hotel, St Leonards.

       [CHARLES *in his wheelchair. Rug over his knees. Sound of waves.*
       TOM *has a sheaf of pages.* ROSE *stops him for a moment.*]

ROSE: He doesn't understand. Just talk to him. He likes that. He's
grown very fond of you.

       [*She goes.*]

CHARLES: Let me guess. It's that poem.

       [TOM *folds the pages away. He listens to the waves.*]

TOM: ... I think I spent half my childhood listening to the sea. Of
course I was raised in St Louis. But then Dad built a summer
house in New England for the vacation. Right on the bay. So
life was always in two halves. In St Louis I missed the blue
waters of Maine and when I was on the Cape I missed the
old city of cinder stacks in the midwest.

     ... And so these two parts of me formed a kind of divide.
I look towards America and it is barren. I live to be a European
and discover corruption.

     ... I think you ought to know I owe you my life. The job
at the bank. The clothes. The kindnesses. Well, I believe family
is the root of culture. I grew up to think it wrong to buy candy
for oneself alone. Oh, I can hear laughter in the coral kingdom.
I know they sniff in their patent socks about this rather dull
Yankee. But you can have no idea what a privilege it is to
become a European.

       [CHARLES *settles in his chair.*]

     ... And I still cannot put these two halves together. I am the
clerk in the Foreign and Colonial Section who imagines he's
a poet. I am a poet at night who hopes to achieve the rank
of branch manager. But I'm afraid the clerk is almost destroyed
with the idea that he will never write anything of lasting
value. Despair eats into him. It's like a man who gets vertigo
on a doorstep. He wants to fall. But in despair there is no
gravity ... Charles?

       [*The old man seems to sleep.*]

     ... I have asked the bank for three months' leave of absence.

In order to write. It is entirely an artistic decision. And
Vivienne wants this, too. She knows that we cannot go on like
this. She knows that we cannot go on like this.

[TOM *stands to leave. He watches* CHARLES. CHARLES's *head is
low.* TOM *moves away.* CHARLES *lifts his head slowly.* TOM
turns.]

CHARLES [*tired and frail*]: I'd never interfere, but what have you both
done to each other?

[TOM *still. Lights.*]

RAM

ROSE   [*introduces*]: PART THREE 1927

3 Compayne Gardens.

[MAURICE *walks towards us. Dark suit and black tie.*]

MAURICE: Tom got Lady Rothermere to help him start a magazine. Not for the likes of myself. I shot off to Kenya. Sort of start a new life. I never thought about home until Christmas turned up. Pangs a bit. After five turned up it really did pang. Then dear old Dad died. Just got back from Happy Valley to sort out the will.

[ROSE *and* TOM *and* MAURICE *exchange a number of documents. They are in mourning.*]

TOM: Maurice.

MAURICE: ... Easy peasy, Mums. That's it.

ROSE: You do know — I've no idea what your father pays the servants. I don't think I've ever seen the baker's boy.

TOM: I'll have it all dealt with. You won't have to think about details. The trust fund pays for the upkeep of the house.

ROSE: What do we tell Vivie?

MAURICE: Not a lot.

ROSE: Is that the form?

TOM: I don't want to overburden her.

ROSE: Well, of course, her saving grace is she knows nothing about money. And is entirely uninterested in the contents of a will.

[VIVIENNE *enters. Black voile swagger, hat and scarf.*]

... There you are.

VIVIENNE: ... Mums.

ROSE: Looking so lovely.

VIVIENNE: Why, thank you.

ROSE: Such a nice day. I thought you were in Selfridges.

VIVIENNE: What has Daddy left? How much is my share?

ROSE: Vivie!

VIVIENNE: I can't loiter around. Nor can Tom. There's a perfectly dear little house in Chester Terrace. And Tom needs a motor car.

MAURICE: We were talking about Mum's evenings. She's going to be jolly lonely.

VIVIENNE: Oh pi.

MAURICE: And I've proposed she ought to play more bridge.

VIVIENNE [*holds up a document*]: What's this?

TOM [*takes it back*]: Your father has asked for the studio contents to be destroyed. Some ninety-eight landscapes of Anglesey. Two hundred etchings of cows on Hampstead pond.

VIVIENNE: Cows on the pond?

MAURICE: Art – Vivie – art.

ROSE: Charles liked to repeat himself. Think of Landseer's 'Antlers', he would say. He wanted people to glance at a picture across a room and say, 'Of course, Haigh-Wood, Anglesey.' And not to have to think about it again.

VIVIENNE: How much?

ROSE: Oh dear.

VIVIENNE: What is in the will?

TOM [*takes out a document*]: ... Fourteen residential villas in Dublin. All let. The manor house on Anglesey. And this house. Twenty thousand pounds of shares held in trust. A Lanchester Sedan. There is one outstanding loan to the estate – a thousand pounds from Maurice.

VIVIENNE: I mean – when it's all added up.

TOM: We don't add it up. That's the point.

VIVIENNE: However – there's just three of us left. Tom's best friend is the Bishop of Oxford. He has to keep up appearances. The dear boy eats sandwiches. Well, that must stop.

TOM [*holding up document*]: All this must be protected. In order to minimize death duties. Everything stays in trust. The family becomes tenants-in-common.

VIVIENNE: Just tell me –

TOM: I have –

VIVIENNE: How much is mine now?

MAURICE: She won't understand.

ROSE: Darling – not as much as you'd think.

VIVIENNE: Not?

ROSE: You see – your father didn't want you to be bothered with

awful papers. So what he has done — he's not said anything about you in the will. You do understand?

[VIVIENNE *is silent.*]

So that when it comes to paying such boring items like doctors fees and nursing homes, we do it for you. Just like we've always done.

TOM: It is a residuary trust. You are all tenants. The trustees have power of attorney.

VIVIENNE: Who are they?

TOM: Maurice and myself.

VIVIENNE: So — so it's all right. It's still all right. The house and the car and the bills?

TOM: No. The trustee's job is not to line his own pocket.

ROSE: Darling, the boys know best.

VIVIENNE: I have a right to some of Daddy's money!

MAURICE: The solicitor says there is no money.

VIVIENNE: Well, there's a thousand to begin with. You owe that don't you? What was it for? A new brain? Well, it sounds expensive.

MAURICE: I borrowed from Dad to go to Kenya.

VIVIENNE: Will you pay it back?

MAURICE: When I can. It's not so easy just to pick it up and —

VIVIENNE: Oh? Where is it?

MAURICE: I bought a small coffee plantation from this chap in Nairobi.

VIVIENNE: Can't be bad.

MAURICE: It's on Mount Kenya.

VIVIENNE: Sounds bliss.

MAURICE: I — was a bit green at the time.

VIVIENNE: Really!

MAURICE: I — rather rushed it.

VIVIENNE   [*pressing*]: Did you?

MAURICE   [*stiffly*]: There — are no coffee plantations on Mount Kenya ... Bit too steep ... One grows coffee sort of below Mount Kenya. I — I'm in the process of suing this chap. But the solicitor says Africa's a pretty big place.

VIVIENNE: The moment I walked in. Oh, money sweats. Each one of you. The trustees. Is the solicitor informed of Maurice's wide farming experience? There must be a saner way of losing a thousand pounds than tossing it down a fog-covered vertical slope somewhere in Africa. And Tom agrees with me.

TOM: Tom doesn't.

VIVIENNE: As — as — for Tom. We haven't yet discussed the strange case of his sandwiches. God knows I'm tired of making them. God also knows he takes them to church each day. And ploughs through the cheese and pickle on his knees. Have we taken legal advice on these business lunches?

TOM: I think Vivie would like to go home.

VIVIENNE: But, but — there are times I understand I cannot go home. When I'm not allowed in the same room. One can't talk with the Bishop of Oxford with all this going on. And a man of Tom's stature. He can't talk about entering the Church of England when all I want to do is get inside Selfridges before late closing. But should I be told the date of Tom's baptism? Who will be the godparents? Has the solicitor begun to explore the fact that we sleep in separate rooms? And that possibly I've actually driven Tom to this?

TOM [ice cold]: You have not.

VIVIENNE [to TOM]: You could let me keep that. At least it is something, isn't it?

[TOM is silent.]

Quite right. If a baby wants to stick his head in a bowl and get his hair wet it's called baptism. If I want to do it — it's called shampoo. But when a man of forty. Suspicion stirs. We must take this into account. Something new to give the solicitor. Along with lunches. I am not allowed to publish my own poems under my own name in the Criterion.

TOM: Not true.

[Silence.]

TOM: Darling . . .

[She takes a chair. VIVIENNE settles. ROSE strokes her hair.]

ROSE: You'll find the solicitor knows about everything. Knows about the coffee plantation. And the best way to keep the money intact. I'm sure he even knows something about Tom's sandwiches.

VIVIENNE: Oh I see. I'm ill, am I?

ROSE: Of course you're not.

VIVIENNE: No, no. I can hear myself. I know perfectly clearly what I'm
            saying. So let's not start an awful scene. Just carry on between
            you. As if I never came in. Please.

            [*Pause. Unspoken glance. The untaken step. A scuttling sideways.*]

MAURICE: ... Bridge?

            [*Lights.*]

---

24 Russell Square.

[TOM *rifles through a box of chocolates. It is the office of the*
Criterion *above Faber & Gwyer.* TOM's *New England accent
has vanished.*]

VIVIENNE: ... None left?

TOM: Question: If God walked in the door. Collected poems of Bill
            Carlos Williams in one hand, box of Cadbury's best in the
            other, he said you had one choice, you could take the poems
            to Heaven or eat the chocolates in Hell. What would you take?

VIVIENNE: The poems.

TOM: Absolutely.

            [*The chocolate box is empty.*

            TOM *tips the brown paper cups on to the floor.*]

TOM: Letter.

            [VIV *writes.*]

            Brethren House
            Llanidloes
            Radnorshire
            To the Editor of the *Criterion*
            Dear Sir,
            According to Mr T. S. Eliot one cannot observe sin without
            confession. And man's ultimate goal is a series of events, no
            matter how trivial, which leads him to an Act of Faith.
            Sir, as a lay preacher for the Free Wesleyan Chapel of
            Wales, may I protest? Faith, Mr Eliot, is not an obstacle course
            for pin cushions.
            Yours etc.
            Dr Charles Augustus Grimble

VIVIENNE: Wonderful!

[MAURICE *enters. He holds out a large box of chocolates.*]

MAURICE: Is this the esteemed office of the *Criterion* magazine?

VIVIENNE: Mine!

TOM: Mine!

[*They both grab for the box together. From where* MAURICE *stands it could appear that they are both fighting.*]

MAURICE: One only has to step inside a room with you two and you're fighting. If only you knew what a relief it would be all round, if you could both be normal just for a while.

[TOM *and* VIVIENNE *increase 'fight'.*]

... Mums and me are worried stiff. All very well if a chap wants to be baptized. But at forty. I mean. And if you didn't want children what did you get married for?

... When it comes to grey matter Tom, I look up to you.

... Knew you'd become famous when I saw this article in the Nairobi paper. Not well known massively for poetry reviews. Write-up said *The Waste Land* was total balderdash. Didn't post it. Didn't want to depress you. I met this American girl in Mombasa. Got drinking. She'd actually read the poems. Staggering coincidence! Oh God, I said, snap! That's my brother-in-law, the *fratris.* Should have seen her face. Almost dropped it in the pink gin.

... I mean, if you both go on like this. Punishing, sort of thing. Any broker will tell you the bohemian life is dicey. And these top people in book circles will put their money on other horses.

VIVIENNE   [*dictates*]: Letter.

Working Women's Association

Hampstead Village

Hampstead

Dear *Criterion*

The enslaved women of Hampstead cry out!

TOM   [*writing*]: Onward.

Allen & Hanbury's chemist, Finchley Road.

[LOUISE *speaks to an assistant.*]

LOUISE: Well, Lilian. It was my mother's fault really. She said – where's your social conscience, you do have one! So I joined the Women's Labour Group. I thought Women for Socialism had a point.

[*She sees* TOM. *She steps forward and takes the prescription from him.*]

Thank you, sir. Will you wait here?

[*She steps back.*]

So I went to this meeting. Signed up. And a hand pops up and asks for a halfpenny sub. Oh, there goes my bus fare! On to the platform comes the former Home Secretary, Mr Henderson. There I was expecting a pep talk about the women. And he announces that the Women's Labour Group is to be swallowed up by the Independent Labour Party! Women for Socialism is one thing. It's quite another when all those men in the I.L.P. barge in and take you over. Lock, stock. Then he led off and sang 'The Red Flag'. I may have a social whatnot but I am no Bolshevik. And the rain was cats and dogs. I walked home in my sandals.

[LOUISE *steps forward with the bottles. Hands them to* TOM.]

There you are, sir. How is Mrs Eliot?

[TOM *holds his umbrella and bowler.*]

---

3 Compayne Gardens.

[ROSE *and* VIVIENNE *wearing evening dress.* MAURICE *in black tie. A fourth chair is empty. They glance at their bridge cards.*]

ROSE [*calling*]: ... Tom?

VIVIENNE: ... Tom.

MAURICE [*to* VIVIENNE]: Tell him.

VIVIENNE: Come along, please. Do come along!

[TOM *turns. Takes his seat. Studies his cards.*]

ROSE: One club.
VIVIENNE: One spade.
MAURICE: No bid.
TOM: Two spades.
ROSE: No bid.
VIVIENNE: No bid.
MAURICE: No bid.

The Lenare Photographic Studios, Hanover Square.

[TOM *and* VIVIENNE *take up a 'society' pose in the studio. It is to be a dramatic half-profile portrait. The* PHOTOGRAPHER *guides them.*

PHOTOGRAPHER   [*his back to us*]: Sir's hand on madam's neck. Madam's neck yearns. Less chin. More neck. Sir's brow is not furrowed. We look intense. In the distance. Far as we can see. Still. Thirty seconds, please!

[VIVIENNE *steps forward.*]

VIVIENNE: A flurry of snow in the sky,
            Cold blue English sky,
            And then the lunch party broke up
            And people said they must go
            And there was an end (for a session)
              of the eternal Aldous Huxley –
            Elizabeth Bibesco – Clive Bell –
              unceasing clamour of inanities.

            I looked at you and you had stretched
              your arms up above your head
            With such an air of weariness,
            Like some very old monkey.

            I looked at you and you looked at me.
            I longed to speak to you
              but I didn't. I longed
            to come and stand beside you at the window and
              look out at the fleering
                cold English sunshine and say,

Is it necessary –
Is this necessary –
Tell me, is it *necessary* that we go through this?

St Peter's, Finstock Church, Wychwood Forest, Oxon.

[TOM *holds his umbrella and bowler.*]

TOM: I, Thomas, renounce the devil and all his works, the vain pomp
       and glory of this world, and the carnal desires of the flesh.
            I believe in the Holy Ghost. The Holy Catholic Church. The
       Communion of Saints. The remission of sins. The resurrection
       of the flesh and everlasting life after death.
            It is my desire to be baptized in this faith.
       [*Lights.*]

ACT TWO

LOUISE [*introduces*]: PART FOUR 1932

3 Compayne Gardens.

[JANES *is played by the same actor who plays* CHARLES.]

TOM: ... William Leonard Janes.

JANES: Honour it is, ma'am.

TOM: Janes would like to tell you something of his background.

JANES: Enlisted Surrey Rifles at age of ten. Served overseas twice in African parts. Served twenty years at Redhill Ordnance. On detachment, joined Lord Baden-Powell's Police Auxiliary. On finding oneself retired, took up post with district bank as night porter.

TOM: Janes is very dependable, and has never had a day's illness in his life.

ROSE: Is that it?

TOM: No. He's served in the Manchester Police. Too modest to say so – he was awarded a Commendation Medal. And presented in person by Princess Marina, Duchess of Kent. There was an incident in the canal. A boy and a dog.

MAURICE: Sort of saved the boy's life?

JANES: No, sir. The lad got swept off. Terrible severe weather. It was the dog's.

TOM: Thank you, Janes!

ROSE: What else?

JANES: I got a part-time job with the Association of Private Practitioners. As a medical officer. My deepest concern is for ladies of high rank who require special assistance. I take it, ma'am, you're curious to know how I set about this?

ROSE: Riveted.

JANES: I make the acquaintance of the family to ascertain its high standing.

MAURICE: That's us. Cromwell.

JANES: I observe the client in question from a discreet location. She may be at a railway station. I make my notes accordingly. I then require two doctors.

TOM: Janes has met Dr Cyriax and Dr Miller.

JANES: The spouse concerned will wait until the client is in need of attention. He gives me a telephone ring. Be it day or night. I immediately fetch round the doctors. The doctors are obliged by law to ask the client two questions of a simple nature. Client being in such crisis cannot answer to any medical satisfaction. I do hope I am not bringing distress to you, ma'am?

             [ROSE *is silent.*]

TOM: And the next morning, Janes?

JANES: Nine o'clock sharp. I brings the doctors to the magistrate. The spouse signs a petition supported by the doctors' affidavits. The doctors apply to the Court for a reception order. And I arrange transport to the home. Has Mrs Wood anything she'd like to put to me?

ROSE: Mrs Haigh-Wood.

JANES: I do not converse with tradesmen. Loose talk with news-hounds is forbidden. Neighbours aware of nothing untoward. If there is one desire I have it is to lay your mind at rest —

TOM: Janes —

JANES: For those of a religious turn of mind —

MAURICE: Good day, Janes!

JANES: Ma'am ...

             [MAURICE *guides* JANES *out.* ROSE *sits.* MAURICE *returns.*]

ROSE: ... Why?

MAURICE: 'Poor Tom', Mums. Christ!

ROSE: ... to come to this.

MAURICE   [*quite guilty*]: Wouldn't you?

ROSE: I don't know what you mean.

MAURICE: This big house and staff all to yourself. You take her in, go on.

ROSE: I'm afraid.

MAURICE: Course you are. Else we wouldn't be doing this.

ROSE [*to* TOM]: Where is she?

TOM: I've sent her to Selfridges. She knows she can go there.

ROSE: What else does she know?

TOM: I've explained it very carefully. I'll be away six months. It's very good money. A professorship. Harvard. She won't be able to cope, Rose.

MAURICE: I mean — we're all in the car — bit speedy — Tom's driving — she throws herself out of the window. Not any old window. The driver's window. Almost killed the lot of us. What?

ROSE: Occasionally she gets car-sick — I —

MAURICE: Come off it, Mums! The poem, the chocolate, the bedlinen. The man's career is at stake. Gives a lecture at the Lambeth Palace. All go up in smoke in no time.

TOM: Maurice —

MAURICE: No, no. Short memory these top people. One slip with a wonky squaw. Big stab in the back. The man can't go anywhere. Or take her anywhere. What's she doing now? She's running all over town with a knife in her handbag. Poor sod only has to say, 'Meet the wife,' and a brigade of Bloomsbury wallahs stampede mad dog for the carsey.

ROSE: What knife?

TOM: Certain women are convinced their lives are in danger. Respectable married women with whom I'm supposed to be having affairs. Ottoline Morrell. Virginia Woolf.

ROSE: Now, one wears yellow socks and purple feathers. And one is a collision between a kangaroo and a canary. I never know which is which. What would she be doing with a knife?

TOM: She's been observed at the station waiting for the Oxford train to come in. She's stood outside a tea-room for hours in the rain. Ottoline won't put foot on Paddington without an escort. Virginia only leaves her house by taxi.

ROSE: Let's just say they are types who have a taste for notoriety and imagination.

MAURICE: What's it to be then? Disgrace? A frightful incident in a public place? It's taken me thirteen years to get inside the stock exchange –

ROSE: That's enough!

TOM: I've gone from one doctor to another. 'The swellings are to do with her brain.' 'The bleeding is intestinal catarrh.' It is far worse than that.

ROSE: The finest doctor in the land. The King's own physician. He said there was an imbalance. Nothing more.

TOM: From one end of Harley Street to the other. Every doctor has stated – moral insanity is a disease of the brain. They're resolute.

ROSE: I –

MAURICE: The scandal, Mums.

TOM: We have to believe the doctors, otherwise we have nothing.

ROSE: I ... you must tell me – it is just for a while?

TOM: Yes.

ROSE: It is the right thing.

TOM: I cannot pretend to you.

MAURICE: And it is a very impressive place. Acres of grass. Splendid inside. Best walnut. It'd convince me.

ROSE: I don't suppose it looks very different from anything else.

MAURICE: Rather.

ROSE: Inside. It's different. Poor baby.

MAURICE: Now, Mums.

ROSE: There always have been doctors. All her life. And at school. Oh my – she was bright. First at piano. First to audition for the Royal Ballet School. To fail there was an honour. And languages. An impeccable accent. So much so, when school party went to Paris, strangers stopped and were astonished. Such a good school, too. And what she could do with the common voice when she tried. Speech mistress gave her an award for the best cockney accent in Tunbridge Wells. Things changed at thirteen. Your father didn't know. Of course not. Her body let her down. And her little mind couldn't accept it. In my foolish way I softened life's blows. When she got engaged to that boy. I warned his family off. I clung to the belief it's so important for a girl to build a defence against the world. Instead of being so naked. Fighting it so unclothed. She used to ... When she was a baby. Something would spill. I'd go, 'Why why why?' She'd always say, 'Cos cos cos, Mummy.' I ... just don't think she can do it any more.

[*Lights.*]

[VIVIENNE *in darkness.*]

VOICES: ... 'Good-night, mate.' 'Good-night, Fred.' 'Night, Eth.' 'Night, ladies.' 'Good-night, ducks.'

[TOM *switches on a main light from the wall.*]

TOM: Vivienne?

VIVIENNE [*tries to copy the voices*]: 'Swipe me ...' 'I ...' 'I ain't peeled them taters yet.'

TOM: Vivienne?

VIVIENNE: 'Ain't but a sniff left of that there gin.'

TOM: Vivie.

VIVIENNE: 'Oo is it this time – Gert or Daisy?' 'Yer up to somefin an' no mistake.'

[*He is hinged. She is unhinged.*]

TOM: Please. Now ... we need to be calm and precise.

VIVIENNE: Oh, there's no need for that. If you want to go out. Do go out. I want you to go.

TOM: Please, Vivie –

VIVIENNE: Really. Do.

TOM: Thank you. But –

VIVIENNE: And it is good for you. You can't stay trapped in here. Goodness, I do know what goes on in your mind.

TOM: Now ... let's be precise.

VIVIENNE: Absolutely.

TOM: Start with the dark.

VIVIENNE: Right.

TOM: It was dark when I came in because you'd switched off the light. And I didn't know if you were in. And –

VIVIENNE: And I was waiting.

TOM: Calm and precise, Vivie.

VIVIENNE: There is no need. I was waiting for you. I knew you'd come

in. And you'd put the light on. And that is what I was waiting
for. I like you to come in. I like you to stay, but — if —

TOM: All right. Fine.

VIVIENNE: I'm being extremely calm here. That is what I was doing. I
like you to put the light on. I like the way eyes blink at the
light. It is suddenly fresh. Extremely calm.

TOM: I'm not going out. I absolutely promise. We'll stay together.

VIVIENNE: I do find that reassuring. But you really don't have to go to
all that bother. Good Lord — if you'd had my day — Good
Lord, it was awful. I know office life is bad enough. Isn't that
so?

TOM [*slowly, carefully*]: Yes, I too have had a gruelling day.

VIVIENNE: Poor boy, how you work. Plays in Scots dialect do not proof-
read well.

TOM: We are going to have to talk about things, Vivienne.

VIVIENNE: Oh we haven't done that for yonks.

TOM: In order that you understand just what you have done. And
what we both must face.

VIVIENNE: I'm ill again, am I?

TOM: Let's start with the motor car.

VIVIENNE: The motor car. Right.

TOM: I was driving along. Four of us inside. We were having a
perfectly pleasant conversation about little matters. My
driver's window was open. You threw yourself over my
steering wheel. And almost fell out of the window. I lost
control. The car crashed. Maurice damaged his front teeth.
You do accept that order of events? That is what happened.

VIVIENNE: Well — not exactly —

TOM: Those are the exact moments, now.

VIVIENNE: I felt a rush of blood to the head. I knew you were driving
too fast. I had to get out. I had to make you stop it. Besides,
it is my car.

TOM: Let's be precise. You nearly killed us.

VIVIENNE: Is the car mended?

TOM: ... Yes.

VIVIENNE: How are Maurice's teeth?

TOM: ... Fine.

VIVIENNE: That was the day. After all. I discovered you'd got the Poetry Chair at Harvard. And it meant so much to you. I wanted to share it with you. And you'd forgotten to even mention it to me.

TOM: Let us be even more precise. Didn't I write it down? On the wall. Now there is no mystery about it. What does it say? Tom will leave for U.S. September nine 1932. Charles Eliot Norton Chair, Harvard. Fee ten thousand dollars. Tom will be back June twenty-four 1933. Does it say that?

VIVIENNE: Surely it would have been nicer if you'd told me. That is all I —

TOM: So as Vivie makes no mistake. I put it there so that Vivie can see it. Every time you go into the kitchen. There it is. Eye level.

VIVIENNE: I mean to total strangers. Have you ever thought that's a pretty peculiar thing to do. We are talking.

TOM: Calmly and precisely.

VIVIENNE: And for the first time ever.

TOM [*cracking a little*]: Ever so calmly.
[*He walks.*]
... So we get to the chocolate.

VIVIENNE: The chocolate. Right.

TOM: The chocolate in the letter-box.

VIVIENNE: I do know.

TOM: We had a fit of pique. We got into a taxi. And went straight home. We got out the largest tureen in the kitchen. Filled it with lots of chocolate. Boiled it all for a while. Took it downstairs. Straight back to Fabers office. And gently tipped all the chocolate through the letter-box. We do accept that is what happened? In that order?

VIVIENNE: Earlier that morning I —

TOM: No. Not earlier. Just between leaving Fabers, at 24 Russell Square, going back home, and coming out again to Russell Square. That is the precise area of time we will consider.

VIVIENNE: I'd had a frightful day —

TOM: Why chocolate?

VIVIENNE: I was so angry at the treatment I got at Fabers. I thought if

I can't see my own husband. The least I can do is fetch him something he relishes.

TOM: The chocolate?

VIVIENNE: You do just love it.

TOM: Why chocolate?

VIVIENNE: I'd rung your office all morning. Your bloody girl said you couldn't be disturbed. Board meeting. Now I rang Geoffrey Faber. Oh, he was in his office. I rang Richard de la Mare. He was in his. Your girl told me a lie. You were there. God, I felt there are wicked people in that building who have you trapped! Slaving for them. So I rushed down to the office. There was a man there who said I couldn't come in. Me!

TOM: The man is a porter.

VIVIENNE: Should be sacked.

TOM: Now you remember you came back with the chocolate. And somehow got it all in the letter-box.

VIVIENNE: I used the paraffin funnel.

TOM: And you clearly remember what you were doing?

VIVIENNE: Yes.

TOM: The postman had just made his parcel delivery. There was a manuscript of poems by Roy Campbell. A collection of essays on *Action Française* which I'd personally commissioned. And an unsolicited translation of the *Bhagavadgita*, sent from Bombay. All written in longhand. All utterly ruined.

[VIVIENNE *is silent.*]

What is your opinion on this?

VIVIENNE: I do think Roy's poems are vastly overrated.

TOM: Let us just imagine what the *Bhagavadgita* looks like after being submerged in a quart of Terry's chocolate.

VIVIENNE: Bournville.

TOM: Let's think what these important essays on *Action Française* look like drowned in Bournville.

VIVIENNE: Fudge?

TOM: I must write to M. Charles Maurras in Paris. I'm terribly sorry. A fearful accident. I beg your indulgence. You do see?

VIVIENNE: Poor Tom.

TOM: It has always been like this.

VIVIENNE: I'll write myself to Maurras — my French is so much better —

TOM: Year after year, Vivie —

VIVIENNE: I'll sit in a corner of your office and clean all the Bhagavad-whatever it is — you won't know I'm there.

TOM: I've tried. The doctors have. Even Bertie Russell tried —

VIVIENNE [stabs the years]: Cuckold! I'm sorry.

> [Pause.]

TOM: Why the chocolate?

VIVIENNE: I only wanted to please. I can't get to you unless I please. You do like chocolate?

> [Pause.]
>
> ... Say you do?

TOM: Yes ...

VIVIENNE: Oh I'm so glad.

> [She holds the Lenare society portrait close to her.
> Pause.]

TOM: Right from the start. We kept secrets. You didn't tell me. I had to find out. People whisper — there go Tom and Vivie. Poor dears. What do they say to each other? What do they ever say? And we'd go home and go through the bills. Count the medicine bottles. Say good-night. And I used to sit in the deckchair by the bed. And watch for the morning sunlight in the hall. You were lodged inside my mind. I'd say, 'Don't Vivie. Please, no, Vivie. Let's not, Vivie' and — We've gone from one room to another trying to pretend we are not strangers.

> [VIVIENNE is silent.]
>
> [Flat.] ... So we must be clear and very precise.
>
> [VIVIENNE is silent.]

About it.

VIVIENNE: All right.

TOM: We need to talk about the knife, in your handbag.

> [TOM fetches the handbag. Places it beside her. VIVIENNE rummages.
>
> There is a gentle but persistent knock on the door. Muffled voice.]

JANES'S
VOICE: ... Mr Eliot, sir.

TOM: ... Yes.

JANES'S

VOICE: ... I 'ave 'ere Dr Reginald Miller of 110 Harley Street. And
            Dr Ernest Cyriax of 66 Wimpole Street. In attendance upon
            my duties. Sir?

TOM: ... Wait.

            [VIVIENNE *gets up. Carries her bag.*]

VIVIENNE: Tom?

            [TOM *is silent.*]

            ... Who brought them?

TOM: You know Dr Miller and Dr Cyriax. They've both been very
            kind to you.

VIVIENNE: Yes.

TOM: We've all had a talk. And we all think it would be a good idea
            if they just come in and see you.

VIVIENNE: Like this?

TOM: They are your doctors, Vivie. They want to do what is best
            for you. They want to come in. Look at you. And make a
            decision.

VIVIENNE: At this time of night?

TOM: And afterwards. They will go home. And in the morning.
            Your mother and myself we're driving to the country with
            you. And we have found a very special nice house where we
            want you to stay, just for a while.

VIVIENNE: I don't want to go to any special house. This is my home here.

TOM: It will be very temporary. There is nothing to fear.

JANES'S

VOICE: Sir?

TOM: Wait!

VIVIENNE: I don't understand.

TOM: I have tried to be calm and precise. You did not quite know
            what you were doing.

VIVIENNE: I know what we've been talking about.

TOM: But you didn't seem to understand what you did was wrong.
            I want your help. You'll be doing this for me. So that I don't
            worry about you whilst I'm away. Something awful could
            happen. There is the risk that the curtains might burn. And

	things can fall out of windows. How often has the porter found my shirts down in the yard?
VIVIENNE:	What shirts?
TOM:	I'd be about to go to a very important meeting and –
VIVIENNE:	You mean Lady Rothermere?
TOM:	I forget.
VIVIENNE	[stabs the years]: Lily Rothermere is the daughter of a blacksmith in Norwood. You don't know the difference between a trumped-up title and real breeding.
	[Pause.]
	Ten years ago she took her bed to the South of France and hasn't got out of it since. She's a tart!
TOM:	It's too late for all that.
VIVIENNE:	That's the truth.
JANES'S VOICE:	Mr Eliot, sir?
TOM:	One moment.
	[TOM approaches her. She backs off.]
VIVIENNE:	... I do have a choice?
TOM:	... The doctors will come in. They'll be discreet.
VIVIENNE:	If I'm all right. Not ill. If there is nothing wrong with me?
TOM:	Then they'll go away.
VIVIENNE:	I'm not going to be deprived of seeing you on the boat?
TOM	[agreeing]: If you can pull yourself together.
VIVIENNE:	You'll let me be there waving you good-bye?
TOM	[agreeing]: If you can just take hold of yourself.
VIVIENNE:	After all, there have been good moments in the past. Just you and me, Tom. We've had our splendid times, haven't we?
TOM:	Yes.
	[She goes to the screen back of the cot. Takes down all the photographs of TOM. Puts them under a blanket. Straightens her hair. Pulls on a dressing-gown. Rouge. Lipstick. Dancing pumps. She stands. Clutches handbag.]
VIVIENNE:	Ready.
	[TOM opens the door. ROSE steps inside.]

VIVIENNE: Who else have you got out there, Mummy? Is Daddy's corpse out there too?

ROSE: We will be very serious for a moment.

VIVIENNE: That's all right, Mummy, we've already had that. We've been very precise and clear. Haven't we?

ROSE: You must see this our way, dear.

VIVIENNE: Really? Is there a better view? I fully understand one needs a decent stall seat for a real crisis.

ROSE: Where is the knife?

VIVIENNE: Tom wants me to wave him off at Tilbury Dock, when his boat —

ROSE: Give me the knife.

VIVIENNE: We are being a bit Ethel M. Dell, aren't we?

ROSE: I know you have a knife there.

VIVIENNE: I see.

ROSE: It is a nasty thing for a girl to take around in her bag.

VIVIENNE: Of course.

ROSE: And it isn't fair on other people. Because — they might take fright.

VIVIENNE: Who are they?

ROSE: Let's just say there are these people. And we don't want people to get killed, do we? We don't want an awful scene in a police court. That is why the doctors are here. And they have a couple of questions for you.

VIVIENNE: As a matter of interest — who am I about to bump off?

ROSE: There have been complaints.

VIVIENNE: From who?

ROSE: Lady Ottoline Morrell.

VIVIENNE: She's complained?

ROSE: Yes.

VIVIENNE: Anyone else?

ROSE: Mrs Woolf.

VIVIENNE: She's also on my list?

ROSE: I'm afraid so.

VIVIENNE: You believe all this?

ROSE: It causes me such grief. I have no other option.

[VIVIENNE *holds the bag tightly.*]

VIVIENNE: Well, Mums. It's all a bit late. I don't wish to alarm you. But I caught up with Virginia in Piccadilly. In the ladies' room at Lyons Corner House. I'm afraid it's all over.

[VIVIENNE *takes a dagger from her bag. Drops the bag. Advances on* ROSE. ROSE *backs to the table.*]

TOM: Vivienne.

VIVIENNE: I'll show you exactly. [*Holds* ROSE.] Got her like that! ... and that!

[*The knife plunges in.*
ROSE *in shock.*]

VIVIENNE: It's all right, it's a trick knife.

[VIVIENNE *shows the knife. The blade folds in.*
ROSE *gathers herself.*]

You have a couple of questions?

[ROSE *nodding.*]

Go on?

ROSE   [*shaking*]: The ... greasy pole is ten yards high. The little brown monkey wishes to climb it. The ... monkey climbs three yards a day. But ... each night he slips back two yards. How many days will it take the monkey to reach the top?

VIVIENNE: ... Eight.

ROSE: Please, I –

VIVIENNE: Next?

ROSE   [*gathers herself*]: Rupert ... is taking his friends to Covent Garden. They have a box. Rupert is sitting next to Charles and on his left. Daphne sits immediately on Charles's right. Clarissa sits somewhere to the left of Daphne ... Put them in their correct order.

VIVIENNE: ... Clarissa is next to Rupert ... Rupert is next to Charles ... Charles is next to Daphne.

[*Pause.*
TOM *is unhinged.*
VIVIENNE *is hinged.*
Lights.]

| VIVIENNE | [*introduces*]: PART FIVE 1935 |

LOUISE   [*forward*]They tried to have Mrs Eliot put away. But each time she
          rallied herself. And the doctors weren't fully satisfied. I did get
          to become night nurse. Took me all of nineteen years. I had
          this little flat for the night nurse above the chemist. And Mrs
          Eliot used to come up and have a nice long chat with me. I
          did like Mrs Eliot. I was interested in her. I joined the National
          Society for Lunacy Law Reform. Gave up Socialism for
          Women. Dead loss, that. Well, her Mr Eliot did go to America
          for six months. While he was out there he filed separation
          papers through his solicitor. And when he come back he never
          went near her. Poor woman, she was off her chump looking
          for him. Then of course they did get two doctors to sign
          medical certificates to support the petition.

          [*Lights.*]

          TOM *and* ROSE *and* MAURICE.

          [TOM and MAURICE *and* ROSE *share a bench in a Magistrate's
          Court.*]

BARRISTER: Your Honour, the family is of good standing and is prepared
          to send the patient to a class of home suitable to her station.
          The licensed house which will receive her is Northumberland
          House, Finsbury Park. Under the Lunacy Act of 1890 Sections
          4–8, I hereby request a reception order for Mrs Vivienne
          Haigh-Wood Eliot of 68 Clarence Gate Gardens.

          I will read out the statement of particulars, your Honour.

          That Mrs Eliot deposited a tureen of warm chocolate into
          a publisher's mail-box.

          That she tried to put an entry into *The Times* personal
          column which read: Will T. S. Eliot please return to his home
          at 68 Clarence Gate Gardens which he has abandoned. Signed,
          His wife.

          That she changed her bedlinen sometimes twice a day no
          matter where she stayed and stole or hid the linen as she saw
          fit.

That upon learning her Royal Highness, Princess Marina, Duchess of Kent, was pronounced poorly in *The Times* court circular, she posted a poem of her husband's titled 'Marina' to the Princess. The poem and its title have no connection whatsoever with the Princess Marina.

That she denied she was Vivienne Haigh-Wood Eliot when she was confronted in broad daylight in Bond Street by two distinguished ladies who knew her well – Miss Edith Sitwell, a landowner, and Mrs Woolf, a director of a publishing house.

That she paraded herself outside a consecrated Anglican church hall ... where a pageant written by her husband, entitled 'The Rock', was in progress ... And that she wore a large placard which read: I am the wife he deserted.

[TOM *and* MAURICE *light cigarettes. Stage is empty. Laundry basket at side.*]

MAURICE: Well, that seemed to go all right.

[ROSE *approaches.*]

TOM: I am so sorry, Rose.

ROSE: After you came to us. You had suits. Handmade shoes from Lobb. Charles even got you the job at the bank. You met our family and friends. I did warn them. He's a bit of a stick. But so eager to be like us. And you were fascinated. You had a place. Then those 'wallahs' got hold of you. The Virginias and the Ottolines. Oh, it's not such an accolade to marry an industrious Jew and write nasty novels about one's friends. Or such a prize to lower yourself to a Liberal M.P. who's large among beer barrels. Tell a Liberal any day from his reticence about his private income. I realize an American in search of us grows impatient. And grasps for novelty. But I don't want you to think that Bloomsbury riff-raff is the heart of English life. There is another stock. One great uncle rode the length of the Argentine on a por.y until he found his perfect tract of land. There are Haigh-Woods buried as far afield as Alberta or Nepal. In unmarked graves. Oh, unfashionable, yes. Fine for a snigger behind Bloomsbury shutters. We have magistrates and councillors. Secretaries of the Hunt and churchwardens. Partners in the fine linen trade. This is stock. It goes about its business. Is quiet about it. Becomes that soil of the field. Quite unexceptional. An unmarked soil. But there it is. And you've never heard me mention our kinship with Earl Haig, the great soldier. And I might add – never before has one of us been carted off in disgrace to a lunatics' house. Oh, you swore to us you'd look after Vivie for always. But in between has fallen these long years. It's what you didn't do. So, now you're famous on a bookshelf. What else can you learn? What is there left we can give you?

TOM: I – love this family. I've always wanted to be part of it. Family unity is –

ROSE: No, please. I've lived out my life in the hope that Vivie would be acceptable to someone. Not quite the moment to give me the benefit of your mind.

         [*Touches the laundry basket.*]

         I'll have this collected. After all, it is mine.

         [*Leaves.*]

         [*Shadows.* TOM *and* MAURICE *light up cigarettes.*
         TOM *takes a pair of tickets from his wallet.*]

TOM: I have a couple of free tickets.

MAURICE: Oh really?

TOM: My personal ones.

MAURICE: Oh splendid.

TOM: Not a better seat in the house.

MAURICE: Thanks a million.

TOM: I'm speaking at Dorland Hall tonight.

MAURICE [*freezing*]: Ah.

TOM: You do want them?

MAURICE: Oh, of course.

TOM: You'll be astonished who's in your row.

MAURICE: Total celebs?

TOM: I'll keep you guessing.

MAURICE: Rather.

         [MAURICE *takes the tickets. Thinks. Hands them back.*]

         ... Awful swine of a nuisance, I've arranged to take a pal to the dogs.

TOM: Dogs?

MAURICE: Long-legged pooches chasing horsehair rabbits.

TOM: I see.

MAURICE: . . . Got a good show lined up for the troops, so to speak?

TOM: It's called – 'Is There an Alien Culture?'

MAURICE: That's the stuff to thrash them with.

TOM: I might have to stay at your place tonight. I don't have a place of my own. Usually Virginia or Sachie will put me up. It's absurd to pay for an hotel.

MAURICE: Absurd.

TOM: I'll take the couch.

MAURICE   [*freezing*]: Ah.

> [*Pause. Certain toughness in* MAURICE.]

. . . Awful swine of a bother. You see this pal's not a chap. He's a member of the opposite sex. I mean – you do understand?

> [*They smoke.*]

TOM: We'll have to settle everything up with the solicitor. Vivie's place. The money. I'm going to have to rely on you.

MAURICE: Ah . . .

TOM: I do need you.

MAURICE: . . . Awful thing about this. Swinish thing. I'm off away. Got to have a chat with our man at the Nigerian Commission tomorrow. And I'm off. Looking forward to it really. Thought I'd give the West Coast of Africa a try. Can't make more of an ass of myself there than I did on the East Coast. Not too many coffee plantations in Nigeria.

TOM: For how long?

MAURICE: Absolute years.

TOM: Maurice, there's a pile of legal matters to tie up – !

MAURICE: Oh you can do that.

TOM: What about Vivie's place?

MAURICE: Just tell Selfridges Depository to take it all away. And sort of change the locks.

TOM: But, Maurice –

MAURICE: After all, you're almost one of us now.

TOM: Oh, really? But not quite – perhaps I try a little bit too hard?

MAURICE: You don't understand.

TOM   [*stung*]: Too deferential when I ought to shrug things off. I should laugh. Not quite up to Malvern College, or Dulwich, or was it Bedford? I forget!

MAURICE: My old army chaplain used to say —

TOM: I'm sure he did, Maurice! I'm sure!

[*His voice cracks.*]

... I'm sorry. Always found it so easy to call you the ass. Forgive me. I'm the ass.

[*Pause.*]

... You know, we loved each other. But with such pain. At what cost. It was all done in such haste. We were always fugitives. Vivie sick all the time. There came a moment when I realized we'd turned fugitives to each other. It was an evening in fancy dress. You remember, you were there. Vivie said something to Katherine Mansfield. Well, Katherine stormed over to me. Shouted out — 'You've married an illiterate beast!' I said nothing.

MAURICE [*flat, cold*]: Oh, rough stuff.

TOM: I don't sleep very much. Well, sometimes the night watchman at the office lets me in early. And we have a cup of tea in the basement.

[*Pause.*]

MAURICE: I say, Tom. Man to man?

TOM: Hallo.

MAURICE: You and Vivie.

TOM: Still with you.

MAURICE: The old sort of thing under the sheets?

TOM: Beginning to lose you.

MAURICE: I mean there must have been a good moment. A single second. Take this American lass of mine in Mombasa. We were out on the Masai Reserve. The old heat gets to you. And I actually rogered her on the grass. In the far corner of my eye I saw this dead buffalo. Right there. Now I've never forgotten the look in that creature's eye to this day. I mean — there must have been one moment like that?

[TOM'S *dry laughter. Unavoidable in the circumstances.*]

TOM: I can't say that there was.

MAURICE: When you think back?

TOM: Not one.

MAURICE: Ah.

> [*The room darkens. They stand and put on their overcoats. They straighten their homburg hats and button themselves up. Pause.*]

TOM: I shall miss you more than you know.

MAURICE: Make me blush. I'm such a chump.

TOM: No. Really. I think the world of you.

MAURICE: I will keep in close touch. Dreadful about birthdays, mind. I'm pretty hot on Christmas cards.

TOM: Remember old King Bolo?

MAURICE: Those were the days which rhymed. What ever happened to him?

TOM: He got a little quiet. Negroes have become somewhat fashionable these days.

MAURICE: Oh. Shame.

> [*Pause.* TOM *studies* MAURICE.]

TOM: The *fratris*?

MAURICE: Brother-in-law!

TOM: Rather.

MAURICE: Greek.

TOM: Latin.

> [*Both smile.*]

MAURICE: Been splendid knowing you. Feel I've touched history. Well, sort of – hung on.

> [*They light up cigarettes. The dark.*]
> ... Tom?

TOM: ... Here.

MAURICE: ... What have we done?

> [*Lights.*]

TOM	*[introduces]*: PART SIX 1937

[LOUISE *sits in her night nurse room above Allen & Hanbury. A sofa and a chair.* VIVIENNE *knocks loudly.* LOUISE *opens up.* VIVIENNE *wears a black shirt and grey skirt. A little untidy. Hurried.*]

VIVIENNE: Evening, Louise.

LOUISE: Ma'am!

VIVIENNE: It's been a frightful day. Couldn't find a hat anywhere. Couldn't get into the bank. Taxis are just impossible in this weather.

LOUISE: But what are you doing here?

VIVIENNE: I ... I haven't come for a prescription.

LOUISE: No.

VIVIENNE: I came here because –

LOUISE: Sit yourself down, Ma'am.

VIVIENNE: There might be police or vile men outside.

LOUISE: Let's take things as they come.

VIVIENNE: And dogs. They do use them.

LOUISE: I'm sure.

VIVIENNE: I'm on the run.

LOUISE: Yes. Now you settle down. And tell me. How did you get out?

VIVIENNE: The home has lodges and gates. They aren't manned all the time. I slip out and flag down a passing car. I've done it before.

LOUISE: Where have you been, ma'am?

VIVIENNE: Well, I went to an art gallery and popped round to the bank. Tonight I had a bite to eat in the Strand, then called into a meeting. Took my coat off. Somebody started to shout. A fearful scene developed. As soon as they saw this uniform they catapulted out of their seats, eyes popping. Couldn't stay. I came straight here.

LOUISE: I'm glad you did that.

VIVIENNE: You are the only friend left in the world.

LOUISE: Nonsense.

VIVIENNE: The only one I can really trust.

LOUISE: Surely not.

VIVIENNE: I won't go back. They want my mind, Louie.

LOUISE: Well then, we must think of something, mustn't we?

VIVIENNE: I am afraid.

LOUISE: Well, ma'am — why don't you stay here. And we'll both be afraid together.

VIVIENNE: I want you to call me Vivie.

LOUISE: Yes, ma'am.

VIVIENNE: I'm so tired.

[Pause.]

LOUISE: ... It is that family of yours, isn't it? ... And all those pricey doctors? ... And there is no end to it, is there?

[Pause.]

VIVIENNE: What do they all want, Louie?

LOUISE: Such a babe you are —

VIVIENNE: Please —

LOUISE: I think they look upon you as if you've been a bad girl. Their friends have talked about you. They're afraid of you, I think. And that's why they've locked you up in a cupboard.

VIVIENNE: What a dreadful thing to say.

LOUISE: Excuse me, ma'am.

VIVIENNE: Where did you learn such filthy nonsense?

LOUISE: I am sorry.

VIVIENNE: Louie!

[Pause.]

I apologize.

LOUISE: I do too. I wrote to you but they sent my letters back.

[Pause.]

... It is that Mr Eliot really, isn't it?

VIVIENNE: Poor Tom.

LOUISE: Poor Viv.

VIVIENNE: I've been an appalling wife. But we are still locked together. I know what he wants to say. Sometimes he daren't plunge. I read in *The Times* he was speaking tonight about aspects of fascism. Tom adores the fascists. He has some reservations. Thinks they're a bit pagan. So I went along dressed like this. I stood up and cheered him. I jumped up on the stage beside him and I said, 'Bravo!' I said, 'Oh, Tom!' He understood immediately.

LOUISE: What happened?

VIVIENNE: These rats and leeches from Fabers rushed round. Then I saw
            this man Janes in the crowd. He's the one who always takes
            me back to Northumberland House. I ran out into the street.

LOUISE: Like that?

VIVIENNE: It is the fascist uniform.

LOUISE: Is it now?

            [*Pause.*]

VIVIENNE: I'm so tired.

LOUISE: Well, you can't lie down with all this like on.

            [LOUISE *moves* VIVIENNE. *Tidies up the sofa.*]

            Here ... let's take these things off you ... Shall we?

            [VIVIENNE *slips out of the clothes.* LOUISE *takes the shirt.*]

            ... Blimey! An' it's made of silk! Where'd you buy it?

VIVIENNE: Selfridges. The French counter. I thought if I'm going to be
            a fascist, I might as well do it in style.

LOUISE: ... And the rest now ... And this. That's right.

            [VIVIENNE *has a slip on underneath. She sinks on to the cot.*
            LOUISE *strokes* VIVIENNE'S *hair.*]

            I've been doing a bit of studying. The law states if you could
            keep out of that home for thirty days you can ask for the Court
            to set you free. On the grounds you can fend for yourself like.
            Now, I've got this friend. Who's got this houseboat. If I could
            just get you on to the train in the morning ... but do I dare?

            [VIVIENNE *is asleep.*]

            You sleep, ma'am. It's funny here at night. All London
            asleep. All these folk dreaming away side by side in bed. As
            if they've learnt to share the air like friends. Folk look brave
            when they close their eyes. Look like they've laid down their
            arms and surrendered. And found out there ain't nothing there
            to be afraid of, after all.

            Safe as houses, ma'am. It will be all right in the morning.
            You see if it ain't.

            [*The door opens.* JANES *in his bowler hat.* JANES *enters. Looks
            at* VIVIENNE.
            Lights.]

JANES   [*introduces*]: PART SEVEN 1947

[MAURICE *approaches us. In a pinstripe.*]

MAURICE: Met this wonderful American girl. She danced cabaret in the South of France. Married her instantly. We were inseparable – Durban, Montevideo, the Tropics. Mum died in 1941, alas. Eventually located London, Christmas 1946. Grabbed a suite at the Onslow Court Hotel. Dropped in on Vivie at the home.

Northumberland House.

[VIVIENNE *pushes a pretty tea trolley forward. Tea service, cakes, a box of homemade chocolate fudge. She wears a plaid shirt with sensible shoes. Woollen twinset and a bright silk scarf loosely tied in a cravat. Pearls. Her brown curly hair more austere. She waits.* MAURICE *strides over to her. Kiss. Sits beside her.*]

MAURICE: Vivie?
VIVIENNE: Hallo, Maurice.
MAURICE: God.
VIVIENNE: It's good to see you.
MAURICE: Absolutely.
VIVIENNE: And you look so fit.
MAURICE: That's Africa.
VIVIENNE: Lemon?
MAURICE: . . . Looks ace here, doesn't it?
VIVIENNE: Oh it is.
MAURICE: And the service?
VIVIENNE: All ace.
MAURICE   [*glances up*]: Stunning chandelier.
VIVIENNE: I love it.
MAURICE: That's the spirit.
            [*They drink tea.*]
VIVIENNE: . . . How was Lagos?
MAURICE: Bit sticky. Kept a few U-boats out. After the war, got a bit stickier. Quarter of a million dark chaps on demob. The powers-that-be were daft enough to make me Chief of Police.

VIVIENNE: Well done.

MAURICE: Then hit a sort of bald patch. High Commission wanted to hold a victory parade. Night before we had a curfew. I rounded up every dark blighter I could find. Next morning popped them all round to the Chief Magistrate's Court. No Chief Magistrate. I'd locked the rascal up with the others in the curfew.

VIVIENNE: Oh dear.

MAURICE: The Commissioner gave me a pretty generous reference in the circumstances. And so here I am. Mind you, full of plans. Sloped over to the stock exchange. Not a chum in sight. Bought a partnership in Northcote's.

VIVIENNE: About time too.

MAURICE: Bought a new car. Can't get enough petrol to run it. So much to do. Got to put Mum's house on the market. Far too big. Got to get down to Anglesey and flog off that place. It's been rotting there since '39. And Mums, God bless her, put the silver in storage. But there's no receipt.

VIVIENNE: You've been so busy —

MAURICE: Oh and suddenly Tom rang up. He's got some funds to invest. Will I help? He's on the short list for the Nobel Prize. Positively certain he's got it. Hard cash up front. I said at a time like this you need to stick close to the royal family — I.C.I., Shell, Gussies.

VIVIENNE: Tom's doing well, isn't he?

MAURICE   [nervous]: That's right! Oh stupid me. Dear old Vivie. After all this time. And there I go lathering off at the mouth. I want to know how you are? How's it all gone?

VIVIENNE: Pretty quiet.

MAURICE: Can't believe that.

VIVIENNE: Quietish.

MAURICE: And you've had masses of visitors. Celebs from the book world?

VIVIENNE: Not masses.

MAURICE: And Tom's sent you pots of stuff to read?

VIVIENNE: They're a bit funny about the post here. Don't like you to receive too many things.

MAURICE: That's right.

VIVIENNE: I've kept all your Christmas cards.

MAURICE: That's it!

VIVIENNE: I have learned to cook.

MAURICE: Practical stuff.

VIVIENNE: Yes, and I write short stories and take my dance tuition.

MAURICE: ... You are sort of all right?

VIVIENNE: Perfectly all right.

MAURICE: I mean, you are all right?

VIVIENNE: Oh yes. More tea?

> [*She pushes the trolley away.*]

MAURICE: I mean you seem perfectly O.K.

VIVIENNE: I'm as sane as you are, Maurice.

MAURICE: That's it.

VIVIENNE: Which may not amount to much, God knows, but –

MAURICE: Oh squelch.

> [*Pause.*]

> ... And you do see chums? A chum drops by?

VIVIENNE: You're the first chum I've seen since Mummy died.

MAURICE: Ah.

VIVIENNE: You know Mummy never came to see me?

MAURICE: Well – old thing, she was old, and absolutely terrified if one of the family turned queer.

VIVIENNE: I couldn't get to her funeral.

MAURICE: Oh snap. I was in Lagos.

VIVIENNE: Poor Mummy.'

MAURICE: But there still is old Tom.

VIVIENNE: Yes.

MAURICE: He must write sort of thing?

VIVIENNE: I haven't heard from Tom for twelve years.

MAURICE: Ah.

VIVIENNE   [*stands*]: I still get tired.

MAURICE: Of course.

VIVIENNE: You've been so kind.

MAURICE: God. Nothing.

VIVIENNE: When you and Tom spoke. Did he say anything?

MAURICE: Only had five seconds. Rush call about money. That's all.

VIVIENNE   [*offers him the cake box*]: This is for Tom.

MAURICE: Ah.

VIVIENNE: It's chocolate fudge.

MAURICE: I've no idea when I'll see him. I don't know his address even.

VIVIENNE: I made it myself.

MAURICE: Look I don't know when —

VIVIENNE: But if you do —

MAURICE: I can't promise.

VIVIENNE: But if —

MAURICE: That's right. Of course!

VIVIENNE: Goodbye, Maurice.

MAURICE   [*unable to speak*]: Ah.

VIVIENNE: Goodbye, Maurice.

> [*He cannot stand. He leans forward on the seat. Tears of dust. A cry. He breaks, uncontrollably.*]

> [VIVIENNE *alone.*
> CHARLES TODD *enters. He is played by the same actor who plays* TOM.
> *He wears uniform.*]

TODD: Mrs Eliot, I am Dr Charles Todd. I'm a member of the United States Air Force, assigned as an observer to the Board of Control. The Board has to make annual inspections of private homes like this one. I gather due to the war years, Northumberland House has been somewhat neglected. Shall we look at your case, please?

VIVIENNE: By all means.

TODD: When did menopause occur?

VIVIENNE: Seven years ago.

TODD: Since 1940 you've had relatively good health?

VIVIENNE: Yes.

TODD: According to this, you went to several doctors.

VIVIENNE: Extremely expensive doctors.

TODD: There is an entry here from a Dr Miller. He equated sanguiniferous discharge with a 'moral barometer'. Can you give me a clue what this 'moral barometer' means?

VIVIENNE: I'm sure it has something to do with behaviour.

TODD: You never asked Dr Miller about this?

VIVIENNE: Wouldn't dream of it. He was the most expensive doctor of the lot.

TODD: You had something described here as 'intestinal catarrh' and something described here as 'a stoppage in the endocrine gland'. What did you feel like at that time?

VIVIENNE: I had this intense build-up of pain. In the head. I was going mad with it. Then it stopped.

TODD: What happened then?

VIVIENNE: I bled slightly.

TODD: Mrs Eliot, before you came to Northumberland House, did any doctor mention hormonal imbalance? When you arrived here what was the initial treatment?

VIVIENNE: I don't know what the matron called it. But we called it 'Miss Pot Brom Chlor'.

TODD: Potassium bromide and chloral.

VIVIENNE: I'm sure you're right. She was very regular. Oh and she kept us quiet. I stopped taking her a long time ago.

TODD: At various times you took for the head anodynes and alcohol-based items, and paraldehyde. And for the bleeding you took bromides, chloral hydrate, various morphine-based items and laxatives?

VIVIENNE: Aldous Huxley said I drank ether. And I stank of it.

TODD: Nobody drinks ether. You did take a lot of paraldehyde, early on. You sweat it out. That smells.

            [Pause.]

            This treatment you had. I mean all there is – is this history of head pains followed by stomach pains and slight bleeding, which kind of released the tension.

VIVIENNE: Yes, I suppose you could encapsulate a quarter of a century of frightfulness in that way.

TODD: There are today recommended courses of hormonal treatment which would have helped your problem. There is progesterone which is a steroid hormone which maintains the uterus. And there is a definite link between the endocrine gland and the ovaries.

VIVIENNE: Really?

[*Pause.*]

TODD: Ma'am, I'm not too acquainted with English law. You were legally separated from your husband before you came here?

VIVIENNE: I'm sorry to say it's true.

TODD: It states here you have a private income of £900 a year, from the family estate. As a certified patient you are not allowed access to this money. But Mr Eliot was registered as a trustee of this estate, which pays a regular bankers' draft to Northumberland House. It seems to me you are paying for your own internment here. At the same time your ex-husband still appears to exercise control of your money. Could you clarify this?

VIVIENNE: I wouldn't dream of clarifying anything to you. I don't know what you're insinuating.

TODD: And in all this time you've been here no one has made an application for your release. No member of the family. No trustee –

VIVIENNE: How dare you. My husband is the sweetest man on earth. He has borne the most awful lies and vilification with absolute courage. He belongs with kings covered in raiment.

TODD: Look, excuse me –

VIVIENNE: T. S. Eliot is the greatest living poet in the English language.

TODD: Ma'am I'm just an ordinary medic from New Jersey. I'm sorry. I've never heard of Mr T. S. Eliot.

VIVIENNE: You won't belittle me like that. I gave Tom the title to *The Waste Land*. Worked beside him on the *Criterion* magazine. I am threaded through every line of poetry he wrote since we met. 'Ash Wednesday' is dedicated to me, should you look ... Each day of my life has been a frightful battle to stay sane. Never gave up. In spite of some. And Tom has had my undying love. And he will have it to the last breath in my body. And he knows. And that you can never take away.

[TODD *exits.*
Lights.]

[LOUISE *enters. Stands behind* VIVIENNE.]

LOUISE: That winter was most terrible cold. My chemists kept up regular deliveries to the mental homes. That was how I heard about Mrs Eliot. She died very sudden. Pneumonia they said. She was fifty-nine. I took it upon myself to attend the funeral. It was in Pinner, Middlesex.

... I recognized none of them at first. Very well dressed. I kept my distance. And the vicar said these words. And then they all turned away. That's when I saw Mr Eliot. He seemed to stumble. Then ... he was kneeling there. This gent with a moustache tried to pull him away. Mr Eliot was with his hands. As if he wanted to dig down, as if he wanted to scratch up the earth, and pull it all up in his fists. Lumps of it.

[*Lights.*]

END

ADDITIONAL SCENES

Although these lines cannot find a place within the text, there may be occasion in a later production to incorporate them.

SCENE A

Study. Crawford Mansions.
[Drawn blinds. TOM *and* VIV *at a desk, side by side. They exchange slips of paper. There is a typewriter.]*

TOM: When my athletic marble form
Forever gracious ever young,
With grateful garlands shall be hung
And flowers of deflowered maids,
The constant flame shall keep me warm ...

VIVIENNE   *[copies out]:*
When my athletic marble form
Forever something not so pi – so Austin – ever young,
With grateful garlands shall be hung,
And flowers of deflowered maids,
The something far more rigorous flame shall keep me warm.
    [Reads]
When my athletic marble form
Forever lithe forever young,
With grateful garlands shall be hung,
And flowers of deflowered maids,
The cordial flame shall keep me warm.

TOM: Yes.
        [She types.]

SCENE B

[TOM *walks up to a lectern. He carries a sheaf of papers.*]

TOM: Your Royal Highness, My Lord Bishop, ladies and gentlemen. Let me begin by making a summary.

First: I'd like to explore a society worm-eaten by liberal views. These views constitute a humanism. And humanism is the enemy of tradition. It can expropriate tradition, but it cannot add to it. Tradition must be a form of accretion. A coral shore where we wade with our weary bones. Where our beings have undergone change. And this change is our very culture.

Second: I'd like to explore the contributions of aliens to our culture. And how, for example, it is not desirable for large numbers of free-thinking Jews to settle here. I will show this is not an anti-semitic remark. Aliens are merely the symptom, but the worm-eaten fabric is aggravated.

Third: Unity in our culture. I have a preference for fascism which I dare say most of you share. My objection to fascism is that it is pagan. It will give a man a job, but demote the church in its mission for the man's soul. And so culture without unity is a pariah. At best an entertainment.

How can we preserve unity? We must explore the inner man. Personality is mere glass which reflects the surfaces of his coral kingdom. Between an unrealized past and an unimaginable future he finds a communion of grief. But there is a deeper feeling into which he cannot peer. He must dig down to find it. Beyond an incised silence. To a depth of light. An interminable wound.

[VIVIENNE *stands up in the audience. Throws off her mackintosh. And applauds. She wears skirt and shirt of the British Union of Fascists. She raises her arm in salute. Climbs up on to the platform.*]

VIVIENNE: Fascist State
Kingdom come.
The Will to hate
Yiddish scum.

Fascist State
Kingdom come.
The Will to hate
Yiddish scum.

Mosley! Mosley! Mosley!
        [TOM *backs off. The papers fly.*]
... Oh, Tom!

SCENE C

> *Crawford Mansions.*
> [*Sunlight.* VIV *and* LOUISE. VIV *holds papers and a pencil.*]

LOUISE: What have you got there, ma'am?

VIVIENNE: My work.

LOUISE: Really?

VIVIENNE: It's a short story I'm writing.

LOUISE: Oh yes.

VIVIENNE [*reads*]: Sibylla, looking round the room, saw the American financier leaning with exaggerated grace against the eighteenth-century marble fireplace. She went up to him confidently. 'Hullo,' she said, but he only smiled. 'He *is* rather unsatisfactory,' Sibylla thought, and, glancing up at him, she was struck afresh by his strange appearance. The heavy, slumbering white face, thickly powdered; the long, hooded eyes, unseeing, leaden-heavy; the huge protuberant nose, and the somehow inadequate sullen mouth, the lips a little reddened. His head was exceptionally large, and not well shaped; the hair thin, and plastered tightly down. 'Yet somehow,' she thought, as she watched him, 'although in a way he is such a hideous man, he has the air of being good-looking, distinguished-looking, anyhow, and I like him, I like him – if only he would – what? What is wrong, what is missing?'

LOUISE: Well, I know who that is. That's you and Mr Eliot, innit?

VIVIENNE: Never, Louie!

        [VIV *grins.*]

MORE ABOUT PENGUINS, PELICANS
AND PUFFINS

For further information about books available from Penguins please write to Dept EP, Penguin Books Ltd, Harmondsworth, Middlesex UB7 0DA.

In the U.S.A.: For a complete list of books available from Penguins in the United States write to Dept DG, Penguin Books, 299 Murray Hill Parkway, East Rutherford, New Jersey 07073.

In Canada: For a complete list of books available from Penguins in Canada write to Penguin Books Canada Ltd, 2801 John Street, Markham, Ontario L3R 1B4.

In Australia: For a complete list of books available from Penguins in Australia write to the Marketing Department, Penguin Books Australia Ltd, P.O. Box 257, Ringwood, Victoria 3134.

In New Zealand: For a complete list of books available from Penguins in New Zealand write to the Marketing Department, Penguin Books (N.Z.) Ltd, Private Bag, Takapuna, Auckland 9.

In India: For a complete list of books available from Penguins in India write to Penguin Overseas Ltd, 706 Eros Apartments, 56 Nehru Place, New Delhi 110019.

MICHAEL HASTINGS IN PENGUIN PLAYS

THREE PLAYS

GLOO JOO
Winner of the *Evening Standard* Best Comedy Award

'Michael Hastings has produced two giant dramatic creations: The unspeakable Idi Amin in *For the West (Uganda)*, and now in *Gloo Joo* a satisfying comic counterpart – Meadowlark Rachel Warner. Man, did it satisfy ma soul!' – *Time Out*

FULL FRONTAL
'Full of measured innocence, sarcasm and spleen – funny and moving' – *Gay News*

FOR THE WEST (UGANDA)
'Tough, gripping, puzzling ... I have a sneaking suspicion that it's a great play' – *Punch*

CARNIVAL WAR/MIDNITE AT THE STARLITE

CARNIVAL WAR
Set at the Notting Hill Carnival, this unnerving and savage farce has been acclaimed as 'the best English costume farce since Joe Orton's *What the Butler Saw* ... Hastings has written a comedy more complex than his successful *Gloo Joo* and, in its stunningly evocative and physical climax, much more daring' – Michael Caveney in the *Financial Times*

MIDNIGHT AT THE STARLITE
'Has something of the tempo of the quick-quick-slow rhythm of the foxtrot. It is an exhilarating spin through the tinsel and tears of competitive ballroom dancing' – *Daily Express*